# Myths and Tales of the Chiricahua Apache Indians

# Sources of American Indian Oral Literature

EDITORS
Douglas R. Parks
Raymond J. DeMallie

This series offers new editions of works previously published, as well as works never before published, on Native American oral tradition.

# MYTHS AND TALES OF THE CHIRICAHUA APACHE INDIANS

BY
MORRIS EDWARD OPLER

With an Appendix of Apache and Navaho
Comparative References by
David French

*Introduction to the Bison Book Edition by Scott Rushforth*

University of Nebraska Press
Lincoln and London

First Bison Book printing: 1994:
Most recent printing indicated by the last digit below:
10    9    8    7    6    5    4    3    2    1

Library of Congress Cataloging-in-Publication Data
Opler, Morris Edward, 1907–
Myths and tales of the Chiricahua Apache Indians / by Morris Edward Opler; with an appendix of Apache and Navaho comparative references by David French; introduction to the Bison book edition by Scott Rushforth.
p.   cm.   —(Sources of American Indian oral literature)
Originally published: New York: American Folk-Lore Society, 1942, in series: Memoirs of the American Folk-Lore Society; v. xxxvii, with new introd.
"Bison book."
Includes bibliographical references.
ISBN 0-8032-8602-3
1. Apache Indians—Folklore.   2. Apache mythology.   3. Tales—New Mexico.   I. Title.
E99.A6077   1994
398.2'04972—dc20
94-12396   CIP

Reprinted by arrangement with the American Folk-Lore Society. This volume originally appeared as No. 37 of the Memoirs of the American Folk-Lore Society.

*To the memory of*

RUSSELL M. STORY

*Who knew in how many idioms the
human adventure is told*

# INTRODUCTION TO THE BISON BOOK EDITION

By Scott Rushforth

Morris Opler's *Myths and Tales of the Chiricahua Apache Indians* was originally published in 1942 by the American Folk-Lore Society. This monograph contained over one hundred English-language versions of Chiricahua stories and contributed greatly at that time to a growing knowledge of Apache folklore. Opler's compilation remains a basic source of information for anyone interested in the Apache peoples or in Native American oral literature.

The Chiricahua Apaches are most closely related linguistically and culturally to other Apache peoples of the American Southwest, including Mescaleros, Lipans, Jicarillas, Western Apaches, and Kiowa Apaches. These peoples are also closely related to the Navajos. The Chiricahua language, with all other Apache languages and Navajo, belongs to the Southern or Apachean branch of the Athapaskan language family. The Athapaskan family, with Tlingit, Eyak, and Haida, belongs to the Na-Dene linguistic phylum (see figure). Other major subgroups in this language family include Northern Athapaskan and Pacific Coast Athapaskan. As implied by the geographical names for Athapaskan subgroups, these peoples live throughout Alaska and northwestern Canada, in Oregon and California on the Pacific Coast, and in the American Southwest. Based on linguistic, archaeological, and ethnographic evidence, anthropologists assume that Alaska was the original homeland of Athapaskan-speaking peoples in the New World. There is much more linguistic diversity among the twenty-three Northern Athapaskan languages than among the eight Pacific Coast Athapaskan languages or among the seven Apachean languages (Krauss and Golla 1981:67). Excluding Kiowa Apache, which was spoken on the plains, Apachean languages are "more or less homogeneous" (Cook and Rice 1989:2). Linguists interpret this linguistic diversity to mean that Athapaskan-speaking peoples have occupied the Southwest and Pacific Coast for less time than Alaska and Canada. Researchers believe that the ancestors of Pacific Coast Athapaskans and Apachean peoples migrated to their present locations within the past several hundred years (see Perry 1991).

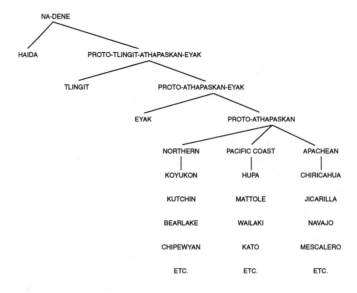

The probable linguistic relationship of Chiricahua Apache to other Na-Dene and Athapaskan languages. (After Cook and Rice 1989:4.)

Historically, Chiricahua Apaches were divided into three bands located in southwestern New Mexico, southeastern Arizona, and northern Sonora and Chihuahua, Mexico (Opler 1983b:401–3). Throughout the Spanish and Mexican periods of southwestern history, despite increasing contact with outside political and economic forces, Chiricahua Apaches maintained relative autonomy within their home territory. After the Treaty of Guadalupe Hidalgo of 1848 and the Gadsden Purchase of 1853, the Apaches were subjected to overwhelming pressures to submit to the cultural, social, political, and economic demands of newly arriving Euro-Americans. The U.S. government created laws and policies supporting the immigrants and used the military to force Apaches to comply. In the early 1870s, the government began to corral Chiricahuas on reservations in New Mexico and Arizona. These actions were disastrous for the Chiricahuas and prominent Apaches resisted the government's reservation policies. Such resistance culminated in 1885 and 1886. In 1885, Geronimo and his followers abandoned the San Carlos Reservation in Arizona and fled to Mexico. In March 1886, Geronimo and the Apaches accompanying him surrendered to General George Crook. While returning to Arizona, Geronimo became convinced that his life was in danger and fled yet again with a handful of supporters. Some months later, on 3 September 1886, Geronimo and seventeen other Chiricahuas surrendered for the final time. The U.S. government held the Chiricahuas as prisoners of war in Florida, Alabama, and, after 1894, Oklahoma. In 1913 Chiricahua Apaches in Oklahoma were given the option of remaining where they were or of moving to the Mescalero Apache Reservation in southern New Mexico: 84 chose to remain, 187 to relocate. Many descendants of these Chiricahua Apaches now reside near Fort Sill, Oklahoma, or on the Mescalero Apache Reservation.

Opler first worked with the Chiricahua Apaches between 1931 and 1935, only eighteen years after the government had granted their freedom. Between 1931 and 1937, he spent approximately two years conducting fieldwork among the Chiricahua, Lipan, and Mescalero Apaches on the Mescalero Reservation. From spring 1934 until spring 1935, Opler conducted anthropological research among Jicarilla Apaches on the Jicarilla Apache Reservation in northern New Mexico.

Opler summarizes his ethnographic research method in his preface to *An Apache Life-Way* (1941), his most complete account of Chiricahua Apache culture:

> It is my feeling that the most successful ethnographic study in terms of what it honestly establishes is the one in which the writer intrudes the least upon the scene. . . . In determining how and when and where the basic understandings and persuasions ordinarily come to the individual consciousness, the primary source must be the testimony of the people involved. It has been part of my method, therefore, to describe the culture in its own terms, to employ the comments and explanations of informants wherever they seem pertinent. I have preferred to use my own observations as research leads by means of which to elicit descriptions and experiences from Chiricahua friends rather that to employ them as final statements. The picture of external movement is essential, but the attitudes and evaluations that surround overt behavior are quite as important. These imponderables of context the informant can best supply. (1941a:x–xi)

While among the Apaches, Opler worked with dozens of consultants and collected hundreds, if not thousands of pages of native testimony, interpretations, and explanations of Apache thought and behavior. Among the testimony he recorded are the Chiricahua stories recorded in *Myths and Tales of the Chiricahua Apache Indians*. He generally worked with his consultants in English, employing translators as necessary during his interviews with monolingual Apaches. Most of the stories included in *Myths and Tales of the Chiricahua Apaches* were told to Opler in English; others were translated for him by Apaches after having been narrated in the Chiricahua language. Many of the stories appearing in this volume were recorded and transcribed in the Chiricahua language by Harry Hoijer, a noted linguist who studied southern Athapaskan languages. The Apache language versions of the stories were published, along with Hoijer's linguistic analysis and Opler's ethnological notes, in *Chiricahua and Mescalero Apache Texts* (Hoijer 1938).

In his publications, Opler makes several significant points about Chiricahua stories. First, there are different versions of the individual stories recorded by Opler (for example, two versions of "The Moccasin Game for Day or Night" are included in the Chiricahua collection). There are multiple versions of stories, in part because they are narrated by different people in different circumstances and for different purposes. Opler suggests that the different bands of Chiricahua did not tell significantly different versions of the stories.

Second, Chiricahua myths and tales are similar and historically related to stories told by other southern Athapaskan-speaking peoples. Other Apache peoples and Navajos told similar stories about, for example, culture heroes who slew monsters and made the world safe for people, the adventures and misadventures of Coyote, various supernatural beings, and "Foolish People" who acted in misguided and unfortunate ways. Opler sometimes used these differences and similarities in the oral literatures of southern Athapaskan peoples to support his interpretations of historical and cultural relationships among those peoples. He suggests, for example, that Lipan Apaches are more closely related to Jicarillas than to Chiricahuas. Part of his evidence for this claim is that Lipan stories are more similar to Jicarilla than to Chiricahua stories (1940:3–5). David French contributed to Opler's Chiricahua collection a valuable appendix entitled "Comparative Notes on Chiricahua Mythology," in which he cross-references common stories and incidents that occur in southern Athapaskan oral literature.

Third, elements in several of the Chiricahua tales reflect culture change and Apache contact with other peoples. Most of the stories themselves appear to be extremely old. Similarities between Chiricahua stories and those of other Athapaskan-speaking peoples, including Northern Athapaskan-speaking peoples, are best explained by reference to their common heritage. Nevertheless, Mexicans and Euro-Americans, for a few examples, appear in stories from Opler's Chiricahua collection, as does Christianity. This suggests that the traditional stories became modified through time in response to historical events—that Chiricahua oral literature is not static. It was probably common for Chiricahua narrators to add new myths and tales to their repertoire and to incorporate new incidents into their old stories. These changes would please audiences and enhance the reputations of the storytellers.

Fourth, although Opler collected most of his stories in English in the artificial context of ethnographic interviews, he emphasizes that within the Chiricahua oral literary tradition stories are performed by skilled storytellers. Chiricahua Apaches participate in a widely shared Athapaskan narrative tradition within which a skilled storyteller with an extensive repertoire of stories is highly appreciated and respected. Successful storytellers frequently imitate the voices of birds and animals, and employ pantomime or other dramatical devices (see Opler in Hoijer 1938:215):

> It is the story-teller's use of appropriate gestures, onomatopoeia, and asides—in short, his gifts as an actor and dramatist, which lend luster to his reputation. In order to keep interest at a high pitch, he does not hesitate to tease the less attentive members of his audience: *Once the old man was telling the whole bunch of us Coyote stories. It was just the time when E. was having some trouble with his wife and his mother-in-law. The old man thought he would have some fun with E. He made believe he wasn't looking at E., but he was watching him out of the corner of his eye. When he came to a part where Coyote has some trouble with his wife or mother-in-law, if E. wasn't looking he'd motion toward him and say, "I guess it's this fellow." Everyone would laugh, and E. would look up. But by this time the old man would be looking the other way and going on with his story as though nothing happened. At first E. laughed too. He didn't know it was for him. But after a while he got suspicious. He kept his eyes on the old man. Then he'd get tired or look around, and just that quick the old man would do it again. E. was always just too late to catch him at it.* (Opler 1941a:440; italics indicate that Opler is citing an Apache consultant)

Long winter evenings are considered the best time for Chiricahua storytelling. Certain myths and tales, such as the "Moccasin Game for Day or Night," should only be told in the night and during cold weather, when snakes and bears are absent (Opler 1941:438). Because Chiricahua children are expected to be well versed in the oral traditions and lore, storytelling sessions are often held for their benefit. Such sessions, whether they are prearranged or emerge informally when people gather to visit, might last through an entire night. One of Opler's consultants gave this vivid description of these occasions:

> It is not an easy task to learn these stories. You have to be patient when the stories are being told. You have to listen very closely. You have to sit up at night when it's very cold, no telling how long, sometimes all night. When a funny story comes along, everybody is laughing. And at all other times you have to listen very closely and be quiet. As much as I have sat up and listened to the stories, I have to be reminded of some of them in order to get it correctly the way I first heard it.
>
> When Coyote stories are being told, there is generally a big crowd present. The older people, before they told the Coyote stories, would say, "When you tell these stories they make you very sleepy." When you get sleepy, they wake you up. They shake you or they tickle your nose with grass. I've been treated that way. But, if someone just can't keep awake, they let him go to sleep.
>
> Both old men and old women could tell the stories. It would be like this. Some of these stories are very funny, and many times the boys of about fourteen years of age would get together and go to some old man's home and say, "Tell us Coyote stories."
>
> But the Apache is very careful not to embarrass someone before whom he is ashamed [Opler's consultant is probably referring here to an inlaw with whom one practices avoidance—SR], even when he is telling coyote stories. If he comes to one of the stories that would embarrass anyone, he says, "I want to tell you, in case people who are ashamed before each other are here, that I am going to tell some very funny stories now." Of course, not every man will do this; it depends on the individual. A man like C. doesn't care what he says. But I remember that most people would be very careful at such times. Once my father was telling stories. My brothers were there, and my sister and my wife and some other women. Pretty soon he came to one of these stories. One by one we men went out and went into a shack next door. You probably noticed that just now I told my son-in-law to go into the tent next door, build himself a fire, and stay there. I just don't want him to hear me tell stories like that. (Opler 1941a:439)

Opler organizes the Chiricahua myths and tales into six groups. He includes in his first set, entitled "When the Earth Was New," stories about culture heroes such as White Painted Woman, Killer of Enemies, and Child of the Water. White Painted Woman is the mother of Child of the Water, who is revered for having killed several monsters that preyed on humans during an early mythological era. By these actions, Child of the Water made the world safe for humans as they exist in the present. White Painted Woman and Child of the Water are two of the most important figures in Chiricahua culture. Stories about them are related to and justify some of the most important Apache beliefs and rituals.

Tales about Coyote and other animals living during a mythological period prior to the appearance of humans are greatly appreciated by the young (Opler 1941:35). These stories describe the adventures and misadventures of an unscrupulous Coyote and other animals, birds, and insects who talk and act like people. Coyote is frequently the trickster whose actions blatantly violate Apache norms and lead to unfortunate results. Coyote is, however, also capable of performing heroic actions that eventually benefit humankind. On one occasion, Coyote is responsible for bringing death into the world (see Opler 1941:197). On another occasion, Coyote steals fire from those hoarding it and then spreads it throughout the world (see Opler 1941:196). Ambiguities and contradictions in Coyote's character possibly reflect Apache knowledge that the same ambiguities and contradictions exist in humans.

Among the important stories of supernatural beings are those about Mountain Spirits who inhabit the interiors of mountains sacred to the Chiricahua Apaches (see Opler in Hoijer 1938:143–46, Opler 1941:35, 267–80). Mountain Spirits, whom Apaches hold in fear, awe, and respect, live much like traditional Apaches. As a potential source of great supernatural power, they can be both dangerous and beneficial to humans. Mountain Spirits sometimes appear in this world to punish Apaches for their ritual violations or to aid people in times of need. Mountain Spirits are impersonated in Masked Dancer ceremonies, which originate in the personal supernatural experience of a Mountain Spirit shaman.

Stories of Foolish People purportedly recount the misguided actions of "real" people, possibly related to the Mescalero Apache, who know little about the world and who completely lack common sense. Foolish People might feed coffee to horses or stand still instead of fleeing when being shot at. A foolish person might ask his companion to shoot the grasshopper that has landed on his forehead. Stories about Foolish People are not only highly entertaining, but also educational; they tell people exactly what not to do (see Opler in Hoijer 1938:146). All Southern Athapaskan groups tell similar stories.

Opler suggests that traditional Chiricahua myths and tales perform several "functions" within the context of Apache culture and society. First, the stories entertain people, especially when told by apt performers on long, cold winter nights (see, for example, Opler in Hoijer 1938:215). Opler cites a consultant's description of a talented Chiricahua raconteur who entertained the people and whose reputation was based largely on his storytelling skills:

> My father knew I. He couldn't fight; he was no account in war. But he was a great joker and story-teller. All used to gather at his camp to hear him. The old men laugh and talk about him yet. My father imitates him, using the left hand, for I. was left-handed. It sure is funny to watch. I. thought quickly. Even the old people surely liked him.
>
> As a general rule the Chiricahua dodge around when they fight. Though I. never fought, he'd talk like this: "When you're in a fight, don't dodge—you might run into an arrow. Why do you fellows dodge around like that?
>
> He'd say things like this: "Do you see those hills? Those hills were small when I came through there a little while ago. They must have grown since. Do you see that mesquite tree? I was chasing deer. Notice that limb. The horse was going full speed for it. It looked as though I was going to get brushed off by it. Then I jumped one way and the horse went the other. I landed on the back of the horse again on the other side of the branch and we went on and killed the deer I was chasing". . . . I. once saved a large encampment, they claim. The children were thinking of going swimming. Enemies were near. I.'s camp was out in the open on the side of a hill. He called all the people, all men and boys, to listen to stories, and they all came. While he was telling stories, he saw enemies in the distance coming toward the camp. He saved them, every one. If he hadn't been telling his stories, the children would have been in swimming. The white soldiers came, but the Apache all got away. (Opler 1941a:437–38)

Second, parents and other adults use the traditional myths and tales to educate Apache children (Opler 1941:34–35). Stories about Coyote and the Foolish People, for example, are used to teach children about the consequences of misguided behavior. Thoughtless and immoral behavior is contrasted implicitly (or explicitly in the asides of a skilled narrator) with the correct Apache way. By paying attention to the consequences of Coyote's negative behavior, Apache children learn the advantages of behaving according to Apache belief and custom. Further, Coyote tales provide children with "explanations of the defects and imperfections in human nature" (Opler in Hoijer 1938:215, Opler 1941:35). Such knowledge presumably allows children to better understand and control their own actions.

Third, the stories frequently sanction or rationalize Apache belief and ritual. Many parts of the Chiricahua girl's puberty ceremony, for example, are associated with and symbolize events in stories about White Painted Woman and Child of the Water. The stories justify or provide reasons for performing the ritual in a particular manner. In addition, the stories imbue children with the proper attitudes toward animals, supernaturals, and humans:

> The child's first religious instruction centers about reverence for the principle supernaturals and emphasizes the virtue of humility and gratitude. *At our own camps, when a child is old enough to understand his parents, they begin to teach him to be religious, to use religious words, and to know Life Giver, Child of the Water, and White Painted Woman.* (Opler 1941a:36; italics indicate that Opler is citing an Apache consultant)

Finally, in Opler's view, some of the stories provide a "cultural safety valve" for the release of psychological tensions and the airing of taboo subjects (see Opler's analyses of Foolish People tales and of Mescalero Apache Coyote stories; Opler in Hoijer 1938:146, 215–16). Opler suggests that it is difficult for Apache individuals to criticize traditional customs and beliefs without themselves being criticized. Using Coyote as a "buffer," however, a person may treat Apache "usages and beliefs . . . slyly and not without kindly lampooning." Further, "funny stories" about, for example, Coyote's sexual misadventures provide a way for people to talk in a socially acceptable way about subjects which are otherwise commonly avoided. According to Opler, funny stories "elicit laughter and appreciation in proportion to the amount of repression exercised over the subject matter in daily life" (Opler in Hoijer 1938:215).

To facilitate additional exploration of Chiricahua Apache oral literature, I conclude by providing a short bibliography of works related to *Myths and Tales of the Chiricahua Apache Indians*. The bibliography includes many of Opler's own writings about Lipan, Chiricahua, Mescalero, and Jicarilla Apache peoples. It also includes compilations of other southern Athapaskan stories comparable to the Chiricahua collection, several studies that summarize information about Athapaskan languages, and some works dealing with Apache culture, society, and history.

SELECTED BIBLIOGRAPHY

Basso, Keith H.
1966    *The Gift of Changing Woman*. Bureau of American Ethnology Bulletin, no. 196. Washington DC: Smithsonian Institution.

Cook, Eung Do, and Keren D. Rice, eds.
1989    *Athapaskan Linguistics: Current Perspectives on a Language Family.* Berlin: Mouton de Gruyter.

Goddard, Pliny Earle
1911    *Jicarilla Apache Texts.* Anthropological Papers, vol. 8. New York: American Museum of Natural History.

1918    *Myths and Tales from the San Carlos Apache.* Anthropological Papers, vol. 24, part 1. New York: American Museum of Natural History.

1919a   *Myths and Tales from the White Mountain Apache.* Anthropological Papers, vol. 24, part 2. New York: American Museum of Natural History.

1919b   *San Carlos Apache Texts.* Anthropological Papers, vol. 24, part 3. New York: American Museum of Natural History.

1920    *White Mountain Apache Texts.* Anthropological Papers, vol. 24, part 4. New York: American Museum of Natural History.

1934    *Navajo Texts.* Anthropological Papers, vol. 34, part 1. New York: American Museum of Natural History.

Goodwin, Grenville
1939    *Myths and Tales of the White Mountain Apache.* Memoirs of the American Folk-Lore Society, vol. 33. New York: J. J. Augustin.

1942    *The Social Organization of the Western Apache.* Chicago: University of Chicago Press. (2nd ed., University of Arizona Press, Tucson, 1969.)

Hoijer, Harry
1938    *Chiricahua and Mescalero Apache Texts.* With ethnological notes by Morris E. Opler. Chicago: University of Chicago Press.

Krauss, Michael E., and Victor Golla
1981    "Northern Athapaskan languages." In *Handbook of North American Indians.* Edited by William C. Sturtevant. Vol. 6, *Subarctic,* edited by June Helm. Washington DC: Smithsonian Institution.

Matthews, Washington
1897    *Navaho Legends.* Memoirs of the American Folk-Lore Society, vol. 5. Menasha WI: George Banta.

Opler, Morris E.
1936a   "An Interpretation of Ambivalence of Two American Indian Tribes," *Journal of Social Psychology* 7:82–116.

1936b   "The Kinship Systems of the Southern Athapaskan-Speaking Tribes," *American Anthropologist* 38(4): 620–33.

1936c  "A Summary of Jicarilla Apache Culture," *American Anthropologist* 38(2): 202–23.

1937  "An Outline of Chiricahua Apache Social Organization." In *Social Anthropology of North American Indian Tribes,* edited by F. Eggan. Chicago: University of Chicago Press.

1938a  *Dirty Boy: A Jicarilla Tale of Raid and War.* Memoirs of the American Anthropological Association, no. 52. Menasha WI: American Anthropological Association.

1938b  *Myths and Tales of the Jicarilla Apache Indians.* Memoirs of the American Folk-Lore Society, vol. 31. New York: G. E. Stechert.

1940  *Myths and Legends of the Lipan Apache Indians.* Memoirs of the American Folk-Lore Society, vol. 36. New York: J. J. Augustin.

1941a  *An Apache Way of Life: The Economic, Social, and Religious Institutions of the Chiricahua Indians.* Chicago: University of Chicago Press.

1941b  "A Jicarilla Apache Expedition and Scalp Dance," *Journal of American Folklore* 54:10–23.

1942  *Myths and Tales of the Chiricahua Apache Indians.* Memoirs of the American Folk-Lore Society, vol. 37. Menasha WI: George Banta.

1943  *The Character and Derivation of the Jicarilla Holiness Rite.* University of New Mexico Bulletin, Anthropological Series, vol. 4, no. 3. Albuquerque: University of New Mexico Press.

1944  "The Jicarilla Apache ceremonial Relay Race," *American Anthropologist* 46(1): 75–97.

1945a  "The Lipan Apache Death Complex and Its Extensions," *Southwestern Journal of Anthropology* 1:122–41.

1945b  "Themes as Dynamic Forces in Culture," *American Journal of Sociology* 51:198–206.

1946a  *Childhood and Youth in Jicarilla Apache Society.* Los Angeles: The Southwest Museum.

1946b  "Mountain Spirits of the Chiricahua Apache," *Masterkey* 20:125–31.

1946c  "The Slaying of the Monsters, a Mescalero Apache Myth." *El Palacio* (magazine of the Museum of New Mexico) 53:215–25, 242–58.

1947a  "Myth and Practice in Jicarilla Apache Eschatology," *Journal of American Folklore* 73:133–258.

1947b  "Mythology and Folk Belief in the Maintenance of Jicarilla Apache Tribal Endogamy," *Journal of American Folklore* 60:126–29.

1947c    "Notes on Chiricahua Apache Culture. I: Supernatural Power and the Shaman," *Primitive Man* 20:1–14.

1959    "Component, Assemblage, and Theme in Cultural Integration and Differentiation," *American Anthropologist* 61(6): 955–64.

1960    "Myth and Practice in Jicarilla Apache Eschatology," *Journal of American Folklore* 73:133–53.

1968    "Remuneration to Supernaturals and Man in Apachean Ceremonialism," *Ethnology* 7:356–93.

1969    *Apache Odyssey: A Journey between Two Worlds.* New York: Holt, Rinehart and Winston.

1971    "Jicarilla Apache Territory, Economy, and Society in 1850," *Southwestern Journal of Anthropology* 27:309–29.

1983a    "The Apachean Culture Pattern and Its Origin. In *Handbook of North American Indians.* Edited by William C. Sturtevant. Vol. 10, *Southwest,* edited by Alfonso Ortiz. Washington DC: Smithsonian Institution.

1983b    "Chiricahua Apache." In *Handbook of North American Indians.* Edited by William C. Sturtevant. Vol. 10, *Southwest,* edited by Alfonso Ortiz. Washington DC: Smithsonian Institution.

1983c    "Mescalero Apache." In *Handbook of North American Indians.* Edited by William C. Sturtevant. Vol. 10, *Southwest,* edited by Alfonso Ortiz. Washington DC: Smithsonian Institution.

Opler, Morris E., and Harry Hoijer
1940    "The Raid and War-path Language of the Chiricahua Apache," *American Anthropologist* 42(4): 617–34.

Perry, Richard J.
1991    *Western Apache Heritage: People of the Mountain Corridor.* Austin: University of Texas Press.

Russell, Frank
1898    "Myths of the Jicarilla Apaches," *Journal of American Folklore* 11:253–71.

Sapir, Edward, and Harry Hoijer
1942    *Navajo Texts.* Iowa City IA: Linguistic Society of America.

Sonnichsen, C. L.
1958    *The Mescalero Apaches.* Norman: University of Oklahoma Press.

Young, Robert W.
1983    "The Apachean Languages." In *Handbook of North American Indians.* Edited by William C. Sturtevant. Vol. 10, *Southwest,* edited by Alfonso Ortiz. Washington DC: Smithsonian.

# PREFACE

THE APPEARANCE of this volume marks the publication of the third of four collections of mythology growing out of my anthropological field work among as many Apache tribes. *Myths and Tales of the Jicarilla Apache Indians*[1] and *Myths and Legends of the Lipan Apache Indians*[2] have preceded it. Enough mythology of Apachean-speaking peoples has now been published or is available in manuscript form to make comparative treatment feasible. Accordingly, in the useful and scholarly appendix which he has been good enough to add to this book, Mr. David French has brought together references to show the distribution among the various Apache tribes and the Navaho of the myths and tales found in this collection. His work opens the way for a comparison of Apachean mythology with that of other peoples of the region, and, with other types of data, should prove useful in charting the intertribal cultural adhesions of the area.

The materials which have been collated and annotated here were gathered during three field trips in the years 1931-35. My first contact with the Chiricahua Apache came when I was a Fellow of the Laboratory of Anthropology of Santa Fe during a summer field party directed by Dr. Ruth Benedict. My fellow students of the expedition, Dr. Regina Flannery, Mr. Paul Frank, Dr. John P. Gillin, Dr. Jules Henry, and Dr. Sol Tax, have kindly put the results of their investigations at my disposal, and their excellent comparative material has made the task of preparing this volume much easier. While I have tried to use, wherever possible, tales that I myself have collected, the myths obtained by other members of the party (particularly Dr. Flannery and Dr. Henry) have been of signal value in recovering additional material, in providing research leads, in establishing variation within patterns, and in adding to the comparative notes with which these tales are annotated. And despite a longer stay and the opportunity for intensive research, there are tales obtained by others which I did not succeed in duplicating—for instance, V, D, 1 recorded by Dr. Jules Henry.

Besides the Laboratory of Anthropology and the members of its field party, thanks are due the Council for Research in the Social Sciences of Columbia University, the National Research Council, the Social Science Research Council, the Southwest Society, and the Social Science Research Committee and the Department of Anthropology of the University of Chicago for fellowships, grants, and financial support during the period of research. To Dr. Ruth Benedict and Dr. Elsie Clews Parsons, whose encouragement from the time of field work through the period of writing has been continuous, I am especially

[1] Memoir of the American Folk-Lore Society, Vol. XXXI, 1938.
[2] Memoir of the American Folk-Lore Society, Vol. XXXVI, 1940.

grateful. Dr. Parsons' generosity has made possible the publication of this volume. Dr. Harry Hoijer has given me the benefit of his broad knowledge of the Apachean languages on many occasions during the preparation of the manuscript. For assistance in preparing these tales for publication, I am indebted to my wife, Catherine Hawkins Opler.

The myths were recorded from Duncan Balachu, Charles Martine, Paul Gedelkon, Leon Perico, Chatto, Samuel E. Kenoi, and Daniel Nicholas. It is saddening to realize that several of these men have since died. The last named, the youngest of the group, functioned primarily as interpreter when work proceeded with older non-English-speaking informants. Variants, summarized in the footnotes but not given in full, were obtained from a number of other Chiricahua. To all these Apache friends who assisted so cheerfully, patiently, and intelligently, I am exceedingly grateful.

Following the Indian War of 1886, the entire Chiricahua tribe was removed from Arizona (where previous efforts had been made to concentrate it) and transported to Florida. Later a home for these Apache was sought in Alabama, and finally they were brought to Fort Sill, Oklahoma, to round out a term of twenty-seven years as prisoners of war. In 1913 they were released and given the choice of taking up residence on the Mescalero Indian Reservation in New Mexico or of accepting allotments of land in Oklahoma. Approximately one hundred individuals remained in Oklahoma; the larger group journeyed to Mescalero. The myths and tales which are included here were gathered at Mescalero. It has been possible to establish, however, that the late division of the tribe has not resulted in any divergence in mythology, for both Dr. Harry Hoijer and I have worked with Chiricahua visitors to Mescalero from Oklahoma, and I have had the opportunity to consult with the Chiricahua Apache in Oklahoma and make the necessary comparisons there.

By working with representatives of each of the three bands that make up the Chiricahua tribe, it has been possible to determine that Chiricahua mythology was a unity and that band differences were registered only in regard to minor stylistic flourishes. This is what one would expect in view of the close contacts between members of different bands, and the frequency of intermarriage. Here again, as in traits of material culture, the Eastern Chiricahua show some specialization. Their tendency to substitute Jack-rabbit for other characters in trickster tales has been pointed out in footnotes. Also this band, whose members enjoyed a more peaceful and continuous contact with Mexican settlers than was true for the others, have absorbed a greater number of elements of European folklore.

The mythology reflects common usage and concept, religious and secular, at numerous points, and I have called attention to the most important of these in footnotes. Those who wish to follow the implications further may consult my Chiricahua ethnology, *An Apache Life-*

*Way.*[3] A close correspondence between the activities of the protagonists of the stories and the cultural round is almost predicated by the nature of Chiricahua ideology, for the birds, insects, and Coyote are thought to have been "people" at one time, and mankind is but following in the footsteps of those who have gone before.

For those who can recognize them, there are many hints in these pages concerning the recent history and contacts of the Chiricahua. We are dealing here with a living literature, dramatic and satisfying to its audience, capable of modification and growth in response to changing conditions.

MORRIS EDWARD OPLER

*Claremont Colleges*
*Claremont, California*

[3] University of Chicago Press, 1941.

# TABLE OF CONTENTS

# I. WHEN THE EARTH WAS NEW

## A. The Destruction of the Earth

### 1(a). The Flood

The old world was destroyed by water, by a flood.[1] There was only one mountain at the time of this flood that was not entirely covered by the water. And that mountain is called today "White-Ringed Mountain." No human beings lived through this flood, but there was a rooster that floated on the water and got on top of that mountain. The water almost got to the top of that mountain, almost covered it. Now you can see the mountain with the white ring at the highest point the water reached. I think that mountain is in Old Mexico.

It seems to me that it all goes to prove that the earth is just an old world that has been cleaned up by a flood. The way the story goes, there was a bad class of people before the flood; that's why Life Giver[2] brought the flood. It rained hard for a long while, I've heard, but they don't say how long. Then after that Child-of-the-Water and White-Painted Woman made human beings.[3]

There are things that seem to prove it. You know yourself any man can go through the flats to El Paso and can see in the mountains the steps made as the water went down. Not only that, but many peculiar things have been found far down in the earth.

[1] There is every reason to believe that this short account of a flood is the result of Christian influence. Certainly if there was a flood story before white contact it has been subsequently altered. An Eastern Chiricahua informant, in trying to place the event chronologically said, "The Warm Springs Apache talked about the flood. They think it came before the moccasin game (see p. 23). The bad people were drowned in the flood, the good ones were saved." Another Chiricahua who was present at the time this comment was made placed the flood after the moccasin game. A third Chiricahua contributed this statement: "There was a world before this one according to the old Indians and it was destroyed by water. All the people living before this world were washed out."

[2] Life Giver (literally "he by reason of whom there is life") is a nebulous divinity existing for logical completeness rather than because of the functional importance of the concept in Chiricahua Apache religion. This too may be a result of Western European influence.

[3] The Chiricahua Apache seem to have no one account of the creation of human beings. From one Chiricahua Dr. Harry Hoijer obtained an account describing how human beings were made from mud figures by Child-of-the-Water (*Chiricahua and Mescalero Apache Texts*, p. 13). Still another fragment, giving a different explanation of the origin of earth and man runs as follows: "A long time ago the earth was covered by water. Mirage drew the mountains up out of the water. Birds and animals moved to the mountains in order to find a good place to live. There were no human beings alive at that time. Child-of-the-Water was standing at a certain place and he caused a dark cloud to form above him. He said he was going back to the sky. The cloud enveloped him and when it disappeared Child-of-the-Water was gone. Two human beings were there instead. From these two the human race has sprung."

1

## 1(b). *The Flood (Variant)*

There were many people on earth. They did not know God. They prayed to the Gahe,[1] Lightning, and Wind. They did not know about the living God. So the ocean began to rise and covered the earth. These people of ancient times were drowned. Just a few were saved.

South of Deming, New Mexico, is a tall mountain, "White-ringed Mountain." It was the only mountain which was not covered. About a half mile of it was sticking out. They have showed me the place where the water stopped. There is a circle of white like white paint all around this spot. It looks pretty.

When the flood came the turkey ran up this mountain ahead of it. The water followed and got his tail wet. That's why the turkey has white at the tips of the tail feathers.

When the water started to go down, the people, animals, and birds on the mountain top were saved and increased again from these few. I guess White-Painted Woman and Child-of-the-Water went up[2] before this happened. I don't know whether the people who left pottery and arrowheads were the ones killed off by this flood.

After the water had gone down, a bow and arrow and a gun were put before two men. The man who had the first choice took the gun and he became the white man. The other had to take the bow and he became the Indian.[3] If the second man had got the gun, he would have been the white man, they say.

## B. THE EXPLOITS OF THE CULTURE HEROES

### 1(a). *The Birth of Child-of-the-Water and the Slaying of the Monsters*[4]

Long ago there were monsters on earth. One of them was a giant.[5] This giant killed human beings, and so did the eagles. They didn't allow any humans to live. In those days there was also a buffalo out in the open prairie. Whenever he saw a human being or the smoke of a fire he would run over there and kill the people. There was an antelope who killed with his eyes also. Now these monsters were living, and White-Painted Woman and Killer-of-Enemies must have been on earth. But these monsters did not destroy Killer-of-Enemies. That's where

---

[1] Mountain-dwelling supernaturals impersonated by the masked dancers of the Chiricahua.

[2] That is, went up in the sky.

[3] Another version relates that Indians and Mexicans were involved in the selection. "The Indians and Mexicans were made at the same time. They traveled, came together, and had a big meeting. The gun and the bow and arrow were placed between them. One side asked the other which it wanted. Finally the Indian took the bow and arrow."

[4] See Harry Hoijer, *Chiricahua and Mescalero Apache Texts*, p. 5 *et. seq.*

[5] A monster of great size, usually described as shaped like a man and ordinarily carrying a knife and a basket in which to put his victims.

the story is confused. I have heard many stories, too, which say that Child-of-the-Water and Killer-of-Enemies were twins.[1] But this is the story as I know it.

Killer-of-Enemies went out hunting. He killed a deer and built a fire. He started to cook his meat. When the meat was done he broke off a little brush and stuck it in the ground, then he took the meat and put it on the brush to cool off so he could eat it. But every time, just when Killer-of-Enemies thought he was going to eat the meat, the giant would come.

He would come over there and say, "You've got something that I'm going to eat," and leave Killer-of-Enemies sitting there crying. Giant stole all the meat. Then Killer-of-Enemies would go home hungry and crying to White-Painted Woman. These two were the only humans.

White-Painted Woman was praying. Some kind of a spirit had told her, "You lie down on your back and take your clothes off out there. You must have a child by the rain. That boy, when he is born, you must call Child-of-the-Water." The spirit said, "Let the water fall on your navel."[2] So she did.

The child was born, and the giant came nearly every day looking for children. White-Painted Woman loved this child. She cried every day and wondered how she was going to save this child.

She had a fireplace outside. Before she had the child, a holy spirit had told her, "If you get this child, don't let the giant seize him, for he is surely going to kill him.[3] There is only one way you can save him: dig a hole under your fireplace and put the baby in there out of the way of the giant. And when this child is old enough to handle a bow and arrow (never mind how small he is), make a bow and arrow for him,

---

[1] There seems to be little agreement concerning the relationship of Child-of-the-Water and Killer-of-Enemies. In three other versions of this myth recorded from other Chiricahua informants, Killer-of-Enemies is called an older brother of Child-of-the-Water, a mother's brother, and a step-father, respectively (the husband of White-Painted Woman, though addressed as grandfather by Child-of-the-Water). Moreover, the position of Killer-of-Enemies in Chiricahua mythology is anything but stable. He is the principal culture hero for the Navaho, Western Apache, Lipan, and Jicarilla. Among the Chiricahua and Mescalero, by an interesting reversal, Child-of-the-Water usurps his place, and Killer-of-Enemies is represented as a subordinate, a weakling, or a sponsor of the white man. Concerning his origin one Chiricahua mused, "Now that's something that I have wondered about too. The old men say, whenever I ask them, that it is all in Yusn's power; that Life Giver made Killer-of-Enemies and they don't know just how." (Life Giver and Yusn refer to the same supernatural. Yusn or Yus is simply an Apache adaptation of the Spanish word *Dios*.)

[2] Other versions have it that she lay where water dripped from rocks and allowed it to enter her vagina. One informant stated that Lightning was the father of Child-of-the-Water. Undoubtedly he was equating lightning with rain, for rain, thunder, lightning, and water are considered aspects of one force for ceremonial purposes.

[3] Other versions explain that White-Painted Woman had borne children before, but that they had each time fallen prey to Giant.

so he can kill this giant, and the eagle, and the buffalo, and the antelope. Then when the child is old enough to shoot the arrow let him and Killer-of-Enemies go out hunting."

The child was under the fire, and every now and then the mother would take him out. The giant was around every day and seemed to notice that a child was there.

One day White-Painted Woman had Child-of-the-Water out on her lap nursing him and fondling him, and he was crying the way a little baby cries. She quieted him as quickly as she could. The thought came to her mind that it was time for the giant to come around. Quickly she put Child-of-the-Water back where she was keeping him.

No sooner had she put the child back, than the giant came. There he was before White-Painted Woman and asking her about the baby. He told her, "Ho, ho, ho, ho! I heard a baby cry here a while ago. Where is that baby?"

White-Painted Woman told him, "I'm here all alone."

He said, "I heard a baby crying."

She told him, "I'm very, very lonely for a baby. I'm all alone and imitated a baby crying."

He said, "Let me hear you cry like a baby."

So she cried just like a baby. But anyway the giant was suspicious and thought there was a baby. But he went away.

After he was gone everything was all right. White-Painted Woman was praying for her boy to hurry up and get big before the giant should steal him.

A long time afterward she had the baby out again, cleaning him with a piece of cloth. She was trying to do it in a hurry and threw the cloth right down beside her. The baby was growing larger. She was trying to make him walk around on the soft ground. Then all of a sudden she thought again, "Giant must be coming! I must put this baby back again."

No sooner had she put the baby back than Giant was there again. Then he saw that cloth she had been using to clean the baby. It was a greenish-yellow color. He said, "There must have been a baby here; there is its excrement on the cloth."

White-Painted Woman answered, "No, I am very lonely for a baby. I am trying to make that look like a baby's excrement."

He said, "Show me how you did it."

There is a plant which has a stalk that big bees live in.[1] In there is honey. The Apache eat it. It looks like a child's excrement. She had some of that honey. She put some beside the cloth. The giant couldn't tell the difference. So she got the best of him again.

Then the giant all at once saw the little baby's tracks. He said, "Ho, ho! A baby's tracks!"

You'd think that would be hard for her to explain, but White-

[1] Sotol.

Painted Woman made that same remark again, "I'm very, very lonely for a little baby and I made that track myself."

Giant said, "You show me how you made it."

She made the track with the outside of her clenched hand and put the toe marks on with her fingers. It was just like a baby's footprint. So she fooled the giant again.

The child got to be old enough now and strong enough to shoot arrows. But he was smaller than Killer-of-Enemies. White-Painted Woman made a bow and arrow for him.[1] She was singing for both of them, especially for Child-of-the-Water.

Killer-of-Enemies often went out and killed a deer but he always came back hungry because the giant always got his meat. Child-of-the-Water got a very small bow and arrow. And they set out to go hunting. Killer-of-Enemies kept weeping from the start when they first went out. He was a big boy too.

Child-of-the-Water said, "Don't cry."

Killer-of-Enemies was crying because he loved his little brother. He knew very well that the giant was going to kill Child-of-the-Water as soon as he saw him. But Child-of-the-Water told him not to worry, not to be afraid.

Child-of-the-Water killed a deer.[2] They built a fire. They were cooking the very best part of the meat. Then came the giant, just as it was put on the brush.

"Well," said the giant, "ho, ho, ho, ho! Here's something for me."

Just then Killer-of-Enemies said, "There's that big fellow. He's surely going to kill you," and he began to cry again.

Child-of-the-Water told him, "Don't cry." Child-of-the-Water was sitting right there where the meat was, close beside it.

The giant came up and said, "There's something for me to eat." He picked up the meat and put it over on his side, and Killer-of-Enemies kept crying.

Child-of-the-Water went over there and got the meat and put it back on his side. They shifted it that way four times. Then Child-of

[1] Another Chiricahua informant has the bow and arrow made by Killer-of-Enemies. Still another version credits Lightning with making four arrows for the boy after testing his paternity as described on p. 12. For the purposes of this myth lightning, thunder, rain, and water are considered aspects of the same force. The arrows of Child-of-the-Water are said to have been of grama-grass (probably to contrast them with Giant's pine tree arrows) and grama-grass is therefore much used in Chiricahua ceremonies. Some versions describe the arrows as tipped with "thunder flints" (arrow points found throughout the Apache range which are attributed to Thunder, who shoots them to earth during a storm) or with obsidian.

[2] One informant supplied details of the hunt which are missing here. According to this version Killer-of-Enemies wears a deer-head mask in order to steal up on the deer, and Child-of-the-Water, due to his inexperience, very nearly frightens the deer away by speaking to Killer-of-Enemies as he is approaching his prey.

the-Water told Giant, "You are not going to eat the meat this time."

And Giant told Child-of-the-Water, "If you don't stop that I'll eat you right here."

And Child-of-the-Water told him, "You're not going to make excrement out of our meat any more."

Giant asked, "What are you so strong and brave about? Where is your power? What are you going to fight with?"

Child-of-the-Water had the meat on his side. Killer-of-Enemies was still crying. So Child-of-the-Water picked up his arrow. He shook it at the giant. He said, "Here is what I will fight you with."

And the giant took the bow and arrow out of the boy's hand and looked at it, and he wiped his bottom with it and threw it far away. Child-of-the-Water had to go and gather up his bow and arrow.

Then Child-of-the-Water asked the giant, "What makes you so big? And where are your weapons?"

Then the giant pointed to four great pine logs and said, "There are my weapons."[1]

So Child-of-the-Water got up and walked to those logs. He straddled each one and rubbed his bottom over all four of them.[2] Then he came back.

They were trying to decide how they were going to shoot at each other. Giant was angry. "Who are you?" he asked Child-of-the-Water.

"I am Child-of-the-Water. I've been sent here to kill every one of you monsters."

"Then you are going to let me shoot at you first," the giant said.

Child-of-the-Water was not afraid. He said, "All right."

So Child-of-the-Water stood in the east, facing west. The giant was going to shoot first and was going to take four shots in all. Child-of-the-Water stood there, ready, and the giant stood over here. He said, "Be ready." Child-of-the-Water stood straight. Soon they heard thunder overhead and then came a big log, the giant's arrow coming at him.

Child-of-the-Water said, "Let it go over my head." He was praying to his maker. It missed him.

Then came the second shot. It came straight toward him. Child-of-the-Water said, "Let it hit in front of me." It hit there.

Then the third log came, and he said, "Let it go to one side," and it went to one side.

Then the fourth log came, and he said again, "Let it go to one side," and it hit to the other side. It looked as if Giant was helped by the thunder, for every time the arrow flew, thunder was heard.[3]

---

[1] In one account the giant first displays a "pine spear with a point of pine." The boy walks on this to show his contempt for it.

[2] Another version tells how Child-of-the-Water removes his loin cloth and rubs it on the trees which serve as arrows for Giant.

[3] Most informants interpret the appearance of lightning and thunder at this time as evidence that the boy was being aided by his father, Water (Lightning). There are some refinements on this episode in other versions. Some say that the

Now it was Child-of-the-Water's turn with his small arrow. The giant stood ready. He had four plates of rock for coats over him. Child-of-the-Water told him, "Stand on your hands and knees so that I can shoot right to your heart." Meanwhile Child-of-the-Water was tightening his string and trying his bow to see how stout it was. He asked, "Are you ready?"

The giant answered, "Yes, go ahead."

Then Child-of-the-Water pulled his bow and shot him right above the heart, and the first coat fell off. The giant commanded the arrows not to hit him, using the same words Child-of-the-Water had used, but they did him no good. At the second shot, Child-of-the-Water made the second layer of rock fall off. The third shot knocked the third layer off and left so thin a layer at the giant's heart that you could see it beating. The fourth shot went right into his heart. Then the giant began to fall. He went over four small hills when he was falling, and you can see the piles of white flint there today. So Child-of-the-Water had killed the giant.[1]

And then Killer-of-Enemies was glad. They went over there and ate the meat they had cooked. They took a piece of meat on their backs and took it to White-Painted Woman, their mother.[2]

White-Painted Woman had been worrying about the two boys. Then she saw them coming with the meat. She was so happy that she sang for those boys. She was dancing. This is the song she sang:

> "What a happy day it is
> To be bringing in such good news,
> My grandson!"[3]

arrows of Giant were shattered when Child-of-the-Water made a blowing noise. Another version relates that White-Painted Woman had given her son four pieces of turquoise in order to render him invulnerable. Each time Giant is about to shoot, the boy swallows a piece of turquoise and blows outward, and the arrow disappears. Still another version has Lightning breaking each of Giant's arrows in mid-air. According to this version, Child-of-the-Water had performed a ceremony to make himself invulnerable before going out to meet Giant. In another variant Child-of-the-Water picks up a blue stone (probably turquoise) from the ground at his feet, puts it in his mouth, and blows outward each time the giant shoots. The monster's arrow breaks into pieces each time.

[1] Some informants tell here that Killer-of-Enemies, sure of the defeat of Child-of-the-Water, sat crying with head lowered during this contest. Consequently, when Giant was slain and began to fall, Child-of-the-Water was forced to call to his companion to prevent him from being crushed by the falling body of the monster.

[2] In the version of one man, the head of the giant is brought back to White-Painted Woman as a trophy. The head seemed too heavy to lift, but Child-of-the-Water made three ritual feints, picked it up easily the fourth time, and placed it on Killer-of-Enemies' back.

[3] By another informant the words of the song were said to be:

> "I am happy now.
> You have done me a great favor."

Note that White-Painted Woman addresses Child-of-the-Water as "grandson."

And she gave the high, long cry that you hear now at the girl's puberty ceremony.[1] This was the first time this was done on earth. This was before they made humans.

The next day Child-of-the-Water went out alone. He had made a stone war-club. There was a high bluff on the mountain. There was a tree there and an eagle's nest. The eagle had young ones, already flying. The mother eagle was sitting on a rock on one side and the father on the other side. Whenever the father eagle saw smoke or something human, he would go and catch the human being, and the mother eagle would do the same thing. So Child-of-the-Water was wondering how he was going to get these eagles. Sometimes the mother and father eagle would go at the same time.

Child-of-the-Water was out there hunting. He killed a big deer. He got all the entrails out, all the long ones. He cut that deer's throat and took all the blood and put it in the entrails. He had his club with him. He wrapped the entrails all around him.[2]

Then Eagle came. It must have been a big eagle. He picked up Child-of-the-Water. He put him in the nest. The mother eagle was not home yet; they had both been out hunting. Eagle thought Child-of-the-Water was dead because the blood was leaking through the deer entrails.

Then the father eagle sat right on a rock beside the nest. He told the children to eat. These little ones went to peck at Child-of-the-Water, and Child-of-the-Water said, "Sh! Sh!" and they stopped.

They said to their father, "We can't eat it; it says, 'Sh! Sh!' to us."

The father eagle was ready to start off again. He said, "Go on, eat it. Where you make a wound it gives off a noise like that. It is nothing." And he flew away again.

Then Child-of-the-Water got up and asked the little eagles, "When will your father come back?"

And they told him, "When the male rain starts."[3]

Then he asked, "When does your mother come back?"

And they answered, "When the female rain starts."

Just then the father eagle came. Child-of-the-Water had his stone club ready, and the little eagle said, "There, he's coming now." Just before he settled down, Child-of-the-Water hit him and knocked him off the bluff. Then came the mother eagle on the other side. Child-of-the-Water was ready again and knocked her off.

Then he began to hit the little ones on the head and throw them off. But he left the youngest one, and he told that one, "All right, you take me down to the ground."

[1] An ululating cry indicative of applause. It is often misinterpreted as a cry of distress or mourning by white hearers.

[2] Other accounts have Child-of-the-Water slay the monster bull next (see p. 10) in order to obtain the entrails used in deceiving the eagles.

[3] Male rain is a heavy rain accompanied by thunder; female rain is a light rain or drizzle without thunder.

So the little one took him down. When they got on the ground, he hit the little one on the head with the club. Then he pulled out one feather and said, "Let there be a good eagle, not one that kills people."

Then he pulled out other feathers, saying, "Let this be a jay; let this be a woodpecker," and the bird named grew out of the feather and flew off. So we have all these birds today.

Then Child-of-the-Water went home to his mother. She did the same as before, dancing and singing and giving the woman's cry of applause. She was so happy she held him on her lap. She told him, "You still have two of the worst ones to kill."

The next monster Child-of-the-Water had to go after was a buffalo bull. That bull was right in the center of a big open prairie. He stood in that place all day long. He was always looking for humans or the smoke of their fires. Child-of-the-Water went out to get the buffalo, and he was trying to creep up on him. Child-of-the-Water was sitting in a low hollow. He wondered how he was ever going to get up to the buffalo to kill it. He was sitting there just as lonely as could be and crying.

Soon a little gopher came digging out of the ground. He came up to Child-of-the-Water and asked, "What are you crying about, friend?"

"I've been sitting here all this time trying to think how I'm going to get that buffalo."

Gopher told him, "If the buffalo goes that way, you run right to that little hollow and lie flat. When you see that buffalo running out that way, run just as fast as you can to the place where the buffalo is now and lie flat in some little hollow."

So that was done four different times. Each time Child-of-the-Water got nearer to the buffalo. Then the gopher came back again. Child-of-the-Water was very near the buffalo.

Gopher told him, "Now I'm going to help you to get that buffalo,[1] and you must do it exactly the way I'm going to tell you. I'm going to make my first tunnel right from here to the spot under the heart of the buffalo, and the second tunnel I shall dig deeper down, and the third and fourth under these."

The buffalo was lying there looking around.

"The first tunnel will come out right at the heart of the buffalo, and you will be able to see his heart beating. Then you can shoot him right in the heart. After you shoot, you must follow this tunnel back this way and get to the second tunnel, for he will follow you. Then go to the third tunnel, and then to the fourth, for he is going to keep on digging for you with his horns. Now the tunnel is ready for you. Get in." Gopher told him to be sure to shoot the buffalo through the heart. The buffalo did not know that the gopher was making a tunnel.[2]

[1] According to one account, Lizard gives Child-of-the-Water his coat to render him invisible and directs him concerning how to approach the buffalo without being seen. In this version the tunnels are burrowed by Gopher, however.

[2] Other versions here insert an exchange between Gopher and the bull. Gopher asks for some warm fur with which to line a home for his children, and, upon re-

Then Child-of-the-Water went in. There was the buffalo lying right there. You could see the heart beating. Child-of-the-Water shot that buffalo right through the heart. Then the buffalo was furious and began to dig into that tunnel. And Child-of-the-Water just crawled and crawled and jumped into the second tunnel. And the buffalo saw nothing in the first tunnel and kept digging to the second tunnel. And Child-of-the-Water kept going and got to the third tunnel. Then the buffalo followed, and Child-of-the-Water went to the fourth tunnel. Buffalo got through the third tunnel and started for the fourth. Child-of-the-Water got in the fourth and had no other tunnel to go to. The buffalo came after him and was very nearly upon him when he suddenly fell dead.

The big buffalo fell over four hills. This did not happen in Arizona but in Mexico. Buffalo had white flint on like the giant. The Chiricahua used to go there and get some of this white flint for beads and necklaces. After killing the monster buffalo, Child-of-the-Water went home, and White-Painted Woman sang and danced as before.[1]

The next day Child-of-the-Water went out again. He was going to kill the last monster, the antelope. That antelope killed with his eyes; anything he looked at would die.[2] Child-of-the-Water again sat out there crying, wondering how he was going to kill the antelope.

Then Lizard came around. He was brown, just like the ground. This lizard asked Child-of-the-Water, "What are you crying about, friend?"

Child-of-the-Water answered, "That monster over there who kills with his eyes. I want to kill him, but I am afraid he will kill me."

Lizard said, "That's easy. I'll help you. He can't see me because I'm just the color of the ground. I'm going to shoot my arrow to the east. I will shoot it just as far east as I can. Where the arrow hits, it will make smoke. Every time that monster sees smoke he runs just as fast as he can, thinking someone is over there."[3]

So this lizard shot an arrow to the east. Then the antelope ran over there. When he found nothing there he came running back. Just as he

ceiving permission to take some from the buffalo's body, denudes the region around the heart, on the plea that it is the easiest to pull. The bare spot is said to be present on the buffalo today.

[1] One informant said, "The buffalo wished that his hide, even if he was killed, might bring bad luck to humans. But it never worked out that way; buffalo hide has always been of benefit to the human race." Another account describes Child-of-the-Water as telling Buffalo that Indians are to live on his meat thereafter and that he is to do them no harm. Still another account relates that Child-of-the-Water brought the head of the monster back to his "grandmother" who danced and sang.

[2] In one version it is said that the black mark on the nose of antelopes stands for the blood of men killed by the monster antelope of this myth.

[3] Other versions relate that Child-of-the-Water used four fire drills as arrows and shot them himself. As the arrows fell in each direction, appropriate colored smoke arose in keeping with Chiricahua color-directional symbolism (east— black; south—blue; west—yellow; north—white).

got back and before he had a chance to rest, Lizard shot an arrow to the south. Antelope ran over there and back. Again before he could rest, Lizard shot an arrow to the west and smoke arose. Antelope ran to the west and back. By this time he was tired. He could hardly move. But just as he got back, Lizard shot his last arrow to the north and smoke arose there. Antelope started that way. He was so tired he could hardly walk. He came back slowly and fell down dead.[1] Child-of-the-Water had killed the last monster.[2]

Child-of-the-Water started for his mother's home. She was watching. When he approached, she saw him. She sang and danced as before.[3]

[1] Details contributed by other informants relating to this episode are as follows: The antelope is described as being killed by a rock from a rock sling. In another account he is choked to death by the culture hero. Before he dies he vows that he will kill horses and that is why he allegedly "kills" horses today (probably a reference to the fact that horses may be run to death chasing antelopes?). Because Child-of-the-Water slew him nevertheless, Indians live on meat today. At this time Child-of-the-Water says, "After this people shall live on you." Child-of-the-Water takes pieces of the meat of the antelope and blows on them, naming and thus creating the various animals as he does so. He takes the head of the monster antelope back with him and White-Painted Woman dances and sings.

[2] Variants tell of the slaying of another monster, who lived with his family in the middle of a prairie on a small hill. This monster was able to kill at a distance with his eyes but lost this power when his prey was close. The monster went to the top of his house to look around every few minutes and so the culture hero was unable to approach him. While Child-of-the-Water sat weeping over his failure, Lizard came and offered the loan of his coat again. So disguised, the culture hero ran for the house each time the monster left his task of looking over the plains. At the fourth run he was close to the monster, who, though his eyes made a noise, was unable to harm him longer. He dashed into the home with the monster at his heels. Within he found many men, women, and children around a fire. He seized a firebrand, bade them look at him, and hit each one in the eyes with it. He then killed all but one child with his club. He told the boy, "Hereafter you shall live on plants and you shall work hard. I'm going to make many people of you and you are going to be my friends. From now on you are going to work hard and plant food. I'm going to make another people who will live on wild things, such as berries." This is evidently an attempt to account for the existence of the Mexicans or the white men. Child-of-the-Water reduced the monster's child in size and told him to be friendly with the Indians, who were later to be put on the earth. Then he cut the heads off the monsters he had slain and brought them back to his mother, who sang and danced.

In another version (see Hoijer, *op. cit.*, p. 13) Lizard helps Child-of-the-Water approach the monster's home by falling on top of him at the conclusion of each of the four runs toward it. In this version and in some others, Child-of-the-Water blinds and dazes the monsters by throwing salt into the fire around which they stand. One variant has him spilling a pan full of blood into the flames for the same purpose. By some informants the last monster slain is said to be Prairie-dog.

[3] One Chiricahua informant added to this myth an account of the origin of hunting magic. Following the slaying of the last monster, Child-of-the-Water attempts to hunt but is unsuccessful. His mother tells him that he must not mention the ordinary names of the animals he sees when he is hunting them. She also advises him to put a certain grass under his bed at night. She gives him an ear of

1(*b*). *The Birth of Child-of-the-Water and the*
*Slaying of the Monsters* (*Variant*)[1]

White-Painted Woman let water drop into her vagina and then she bore Child-of-the-Water. One time, after Child-of-the-Water grew up, he wanted to go out. It was raining and lightning. His mother didn't want the boy to go. "It is dangerous to go out now," she said.

"But I can go. I am the son of Lightning," Child-of-the-Water told her.

Then White-Painted Woman said to Lightning, "This is your son."
"I do not believe he is my son, but I will test him," Lightning said.

So Lightning tested him. Child-of-the-Water stood to the east and black lightning struck him. But it did not harm him. Then he stood to the south and blue lightning struck him. Then he stood to the west and yellow lightning struck him. Finally he stood to the north where white lightning struck him. He was not injured at all.

Then Lightning said, "Now I know he is my son."

Killer-of-Enemies was the brother of Child-of-the-Water. He was a son of White-Painted Woman too. He was older. Child-of-the-Water didn't want him to accompany him on the hunt, but he came. Child-of-the-Water wanted to send him back, but he came anyway.

Child-of-the-Water cried to go out to kill the eagle. His mother told him it was dangerous and tried to keep him from it, but he said he would go anyway. He killed a horse or a cow, filled the gut with blood, and wrapped this around himself.

The eagle picked him up and dropped him on a sharp rock. The blood from the entrails came out and the eagle thought he was dead and took him to the nest. The eagles had three little ones in the nest. The old eagles went out to look for more food.

Then Child-of-the-Water got up and asked, "When will your father come home?"

"When the clouds gather and it looks like rain."

"And where will he alight?"

"On that rock sticking up there."

So when the father eagle came, Child-of-the-Water was ready for him. When the eagle beat his wings just before settling down, Child-of-the-Water hit him with his war-club and threw him over the cliff. Then he asked when the mother eagle would come back.

"A little later when it gets very cloudy." he was told.

Soon she came and Child-of-the-Water killed her in the same manner.

---

corn and tells him to put the cob back in the husk after eating the corn. "In that way you will have plenty of corn," she says. These suggestions are followed by the Apache, even to the present day.

[1] This is a shorter and incomplete version, but it is included here because of a number of deviant elements introduced, such as the testing of Child-of-the-Water by Lightning.

Then Child-of-the-Water asked which of the eaglets could fly farthest toward the ground. They said the smallest one could. So he killed the others. He got on the smallest one and rode to the ground. Then he killed that one too with his war-club and plucked out the feathers. As he threw the feathers into the air he called the names of the birds and each feather became a bird we know today.

Killer-of-Enemies had been going out hunting, but every time he killed something the giant would come along and take the meat away from him. Killer-of-Enemies always cried but it did him no good. He was afraid of the giant.

On one particular occasion Killer-of-Enemies was afraid to go hunting. But his younger brother, Child-of-the-Water, wanted him to go hunting with him. His mother didn't want Child-of-the-Water to go. "You are too small. You couldn't do anything against that big giant," she told him.

"I'm big too," he said. He had an arrow of grama-grass. Four times Child-of-the-Water asked his mother to let him go. She refused three times, but the fourth time she smiled a little and let him go.

The two brothers went out. Soon they killed a deer. They began to cut it up and to prepare a fire over which to cook some of the meat.

"Maybe Giant will come and take this away from us," said Killer-of Enemies.

"I hope he does come," Child-of-the-Water replied.

"Don't say such things. He is big and strong and kills people."

"I'm strong too."

Just as he said this, Giant came. He looked at the roasted meat lying near the boys. He picked it up and put it near himself. Child-of-the-Water got up and brought it back. The meat went back and forth like this four times.

By this time the giant was very angry. "What can you do?" he asked Child-of-the-Water.

"I don't care how big you are. We are going to eat that meat."

Killer-of-Enemies was afraid and said nothing. Child-of-the-Water told him to eat.

Then the giant said, "You're too small to fight me. Look at my arrow." His arrow was a big pine tree. It is not said what sort of wood he used for a bow.

Child-of-the-Water showed his arrows of grama-grass. Giant took them and rubbed them along his anus. Child-of-the-Water could not lift the giant's arrows so he sat down on them and rubbed himself against them. Now they were going to fight. Each agreed to shoot four arrows. Giant said, "I'll shoot at you first," and Child-of-the-Water agreed.

When Giant was about to shoot the first arrow, Child-of-the-Water stood facing east. The giant shot his first arrow. As it came toward his breast, Child-of-the-Water said, "Phoo!" There was nothing in his mouth, but the pine tree broke to pieces as though lightning had struck it. Each time the giant shot another arrow Child-of-the-Water turned clockwise to another direction. Each time he said the same thing and the arrow was shattered. Because Child-of-the-Water turned clockwise at this time, the Chiricahua do so today.

When the giant's four arrows were used up, he had to stand and let Child-of-the-Water shoot at him. He tried to make the same noise and he turned just as Child-of-the-Water had done. But it did him no good. The giant was dressed in four jackets of flint, and each time Child-of-the-Water shot, one of these jackets fell to the ground. Before the last shot you could see the giant's heart beating beneath the jacket, and when Child-of-the-Water shot the last arrow, the jacket was pierced, and the giant was killed. He fell over four mountain ridges and the rocks show today where he fell. They say that you can ride horseback through the giant's bones, for the place is the same as when the giant was killed. You can see the ashes of the fire made by Child-of-the-Water and his brother to cook the deer.

After killing the giant, the brothers danced and sang. They went home. At first their mother didn't believe them, but they convinced her of what they had done, and then she sang and danced.

### 2. *Yusn Gives Corn to Killer-of-Enemies and Wild Plants to Child-of-the-Water and White-Painted Woman*

The Chiricahua Apache believe that White-Painted Woman bore a child called Child-of-the-Water. When Child-of-the-Water was old enough he went around in the world. Killer-of-Enemies was White-Painted Woman's brother. The giant was on earth and he killed all the human beings. There was no human being anywhere. Child-of-the-Water was born through the power of Yusn. Child-of-the-Water was born to White-Painted Woman, and Killer-of-Enemies was his uncle.

Yusn told them to separate. Yusn told Killer-of-Enemies, "You go out this way and take one grain of corn and put it in the ground. You will live from that." So they gave this corn to Killer-of-Enemies and Yusn said, "You shall live happily on this grain of corn."

Child-of-the-Water and White-Painted Woman were on the side of the Chiricahua. Yusn told them, "You must live on yucca fruit, piñon nuts, and all the other wild plants."[1]

---

[1] This theme is further developed in Harry Hoijer's *Chiricahua and Mescalero Apache Texts*, pp. 13–14, where it is specifically stated that Killer-of-Enemies represents the white man and Child-of-the-Water the Indian in the choosing of possessions (gun or bow, domesticated animals or wild animals, etc.) and a way of life. The same informant who gave the story published in this collection added on another occasion, "Killer-of-Enemies represents the white people. They live on corn. All their possessions came from the corn. They became wealthy. When the Creator saw Child-of-the-Water again he said, 'You have nothing and just run around. Your drinking water is the green water among the rocks.' And the

### 3. White-Painted Woman Instructs the
### Chiricahua in the Puberty Rite

After the Indians separated,[1] they named the mountains, named the springs, the rivers, plants, trees, and berries. They were told that every new-born child should have a name.

All the tribes were together at Hot Springs where they were to receive supernatural power and all customs. At the place of the prairie branching in four directions they met.

White-Painted Woman said, "From here on we will have the girl's puberty rite. When the girls first menstruate you shall have a feast. There shall be songs for these girls. During this feast the Gahe shall dance in front.[2] After that there shall be round dancing and face-to-face dancing."

The girls were told that the basket was there with the feathers. They were to make four runs around it on the fifth morning with the basket closer each time.[3] The women were told to take care of the girl and make sounds when she ran and to mould her and pray for her.[4] The first tipi had four poles.[5]

### 4. Killer-of-Enemies, with Coyote's Assistance,
### Gets the Cattle Away from the Crows

They used to tell us a story about Killer-of-Enemies and how he got cattle for us.[6] Long ago there were no cattle on earth. Only the crows

---

Indians are that way. The Creator gave Killer-of-Enemies everything, so Child-of-the-Water had to steal from his own uncle."

Another short story that has been recorded concerns the acquisition of the bow by the Indians. The culture heroes are not mentioned in it. See footnote 3, p. 2.

[1] The Chiricahua say that at one time the entire tribe lived in the vicinity of Hot Springs, New Mexico, and that from here they spread south and west and differentiated into bands.

[2] The Gahe (masked dancers) dance in front of the ceremonial structure, that is, to the east of it. They dance for the four evenings of the ceremony, just after dusk, and their dance always precedes the social dancing which is mentioned in the next line.

[3] The basket is a coiled tray into which the ceremonial objects of the rite are placed. The basket, with the pollen, paints, feathers, etc. is placed to the east of the ceremonial structure or tipi when the girl is to run, and she trots clockwise around it. Incidentally, the running occurs on the first as well as on the fifth morning.

[4] This is the high-pitched call, symbolizing applause, to which reference has been made before. As this passage indicates, the adolescent is advised and cared for during her ceremony by a female attendant who is especially hired for the occasion. This woman, who in caring for the girl at this time is practicing a rite of her own, massages and rubs the body of the maiden during the events of the first morning.

[5] One of the anomalies of the rite is that the Chiricahua, most of whom used the dome-shaped hut exclusively as a home, carried on their puberty rite in a plains-like tipi of four or twelve poles (covered with brush and not hide however).

[6] The informant, when he told the tale, said, "This story was always told

had cattle, and they alone knew where the cattle were. The cattle were in the ground at a certain place. At that place there was a big stump.

In those days Killer-of-Enemies was here, and he could turn himself into anything. So he turned himself into a little puppy. And he went to the camp of the crows. The crows were moving their camps a little way. This puppy was crawling around where they were moving their camps. Some of the little children of the crows found the puppy and were carrying him around their camp.

Some older people had gathered around that little dog and were saying, "Kill that dog and get rid of him. Those little things are tricky. They are wise. You don't know what kind of a trick it might play on us."

When they heard that, the little children began to cry. They didn't want the dog killed.

Then the older people said again, "Those little things are tricky. Now to see whether that little puppy has anything good in him, let's get a stick and jab at his eyes. If he blinks hard there's no good in him." That's what the older crows said. And they did it. They made a swift motion toward the puppy's eye with the stick. And he hardly blinked at all.

"Now," they said, "get a stick from the fire and put it between his paws. If he doesn't kick, then there's no good in him."

When they put the fire between his paws, the puppy kicked. And all the time it was Killer-of-Enemies they were testing.

When he kicked, the crows said, "He's all right. Keep him. No danger from him."

The children played with the dog. They fed him and pretty soon he got to be a good-sized dog.

The crows all had horses in those days like cowboys. And every day these crows would get on their horses and go out there to that stump. When they reached that stump, one would get off and kick it four times, and the stump would open and the cattle would come out. The dog watched to see just how they did it; every time the crows went to let the cattle out to graze, this dog would run along on the side where the crows couldn't see him. He was watching the crows to see where

---

about Killer-of-Enemies. They say Killer-of-Enemies must be a white man. That's what the word Killer-of-Enemies means, they believe. Killer-of-Enemies means 'enemy' (that is, 'white man')." This statement offers further evidence concerning a point that has been mentioned before, namely, that the less important of the culture heroes (according to Chiricahua standards) has become associated with the white man. It is logical therefore that Killer-of-Enemies be made responsible for the securing of cattle, an economic good also connected with the white man. A cognate story is told by the Mescalero, but with Child-of-the-Water as chief protagonist. In the Lipan tale Coyote is the chief protagonist (Opler, *Myths and Tales of the Lipan Apache Indians*, pp. 122-125), while for the Jicarilla a young man with supernatural power frees the animals (Opler, *Myths and Tales of the Jicarilla Apache Indians*, p. 256).

they were going and what they were doing. The crows had one big buffalo bull lying beside that stump all the time to guard the cattle.

The dog thought it over and planned a way to get in there and turn the cattle out while the crows were away some time.

One day the crows all got on their horses and went to the mountains, in a direction which took them away from the stump. After all the crow men had gone to the hills on their horses, the dog ran to the stump where the cattle were. He found that big buffalo lying there by the stump. The coyote was with the dog as his partner. They went to the buffalo.

The dog asked the buffalo, "Is there any chance of getting in there?" The buffalo told the dog, "I can't give you permission. That's a very dangerous place. First there are two monster snakes, but you can go between them. All the animals in there will howl at you as if they are going to eat you. Next there are two lions with their heads facing each other. Then there are two big bears. After you pass them, there is a buffalo, one big buffalo, and in the farthest part, out on a plain, there is a dwelling. And the leader is in the dwelling." The buffalo told them to go to these monsters and tell them just who they wanted to see. He gave them good advice.[1]

Just at that moment this dog turned into his human form. Killer-of-Enemies stood there. And that buffalo told Killer-of-Enemies, "You kick that stump four times and then you go in. It's going to open."

Killer-of-Enemies kicked the stump four times and walked in. The coyote was with him. He met the monster snakes and said, "I want to see the leader of this place." They passed the snakes. Every time they came to any of these monsters they would say, "We want to see the leader." So they passed all the monsters.

The last monster, the buffalo, said, "The leader is in the dwelling. You talk to that big buffalo over there and maybe he will let you see the leader, but he may not give you permission."

So Killer-of-Enemies and Coyote went to the big buffalo, and Killer-of-Enemies told this buffalo, "Old man, we came here to speak to you. Up there where we came from there is a big prairie, fine grass, mountains, canyons, water everywhere. Why don't you turn these cattle out there and let them graze? You have them all penned up here with no grass. Turn them loose up there and let them get fat."

Then this buffalo told Killer-of-Enemies, "You have a pipe and a tobacco pouch. Take your pipe and your tobacco pouch over there to that dwelling. Without saying one word, hand this tobacco to the leader. He will have to take it."[2]

---

[1] This journey to a "holy home" and these hazards encountered are typical of the experiences by means of which Chiricahua claim to obtain supernatural power.

[2] When asking a shaman or supernatural for assistance, a token gift of this kind acts as a supplication and makes refusal difficult. A cross of pollen on the right foot may be substituted for tobacco.

Killer-of-Enemies and Coyote went through the herd of cattle to the dwelling. There were cattle everywhere. These cattle were watching Killer-of-Enemies and the coyote. Killer-of-Enemies and Coyote walked up to the dwelling and found an old, old man. And Killer-of-Enemies handed his tobacco and his pipe to the old man without saying anything.

Then afterward Killer-of-Enemies told him, "Old man, I come from a very beautiful country. You ought to have all your monsters, your buffalo, and your cattle up there. I have come to ask your permission to take them all up there."

And Killer-of-Enemies got his wish. He herded all those cattle together and turned them out. While he was driving out the cattle, Coyote was running around among them killing them. When nearly all the cattle were out, Coyote jumped right on the chest of a buffalo and rode out that way. That is why the buffalo has a fat place there, and the fat is brown inside, just the color of a coyote.

Before Killer-of-Enemies took the cattle out, the old man gave him bows and arrows and advised him, "Hereafter when you kill a buffalo always shoot it in the flank. That's the only wound that will kill them instantly."

Now these cattle were all out. It was late in the evening, so late you could hardly do anything with them. The cattle belonged to the crows and these crows were trying to protect them in every way. Now the crows saw dust coming out of that hole like fog. They rode that way, rushing to the place where they saw the dust rising. You know how the crow makes a noise like cowboys herding cattle. Well, they made that noise. They tried their best, but they couldn't drive them back; the cattle got away from them.

While the crows were riding after their cattle they mentioned what they had eaten that day. They said, "My liver! My eye! My entrails! My excrement!" They named all the bad things they had eaten that day. That shows what they usually ate. So the human beings get all the best part of the meat and the crows get what is left. That's what it means.

They claim that before this there were no cattle here, and that this is how cattle came to be on earth.

### 5. *The Man Who Tried to Imitate Child-of-the-Water*[1]

Once a man stole something and was caught by the one from whom he had stolen it. He was taken to a room filled with corn and wheat mixed together. He was told, "If you do not separate the corn from

---

[1] This tale was recorded from a member of the Eastern Chiricahua (Warm Springs) band. The Eastern Chiricahua were the first of the Chiricahua to have friendly relations and trade relations with Mexican towns. Dr. Parsons has pointed out elements of European folklore in this myth and its close resemblance at points to the Big John and Little John Spanish cycle.

the wheat in four days, I'm going to hang you." And he was locked in the room and left there. The prisoner knew he could not do this task. He sat in a corner and wept.

But in a little while some ants came in. "What is the matter?" they asked him. He told them. "Do not worry," they said. "We can do this for you." And the ants went to work. Before the four days were over the corn and wheat were separated.

At the end of the four days the man who had put the thief in prison returned. He was surprised to see the work done. "How in the world did you do it?" he asked.

"Oh, I just did it," the prisoner said.

And so this man was turned loose. He went on the road again.

On his way he met a very ragged man. It was Child-of-the-Water dressed in rags, but he did not know it. Child-of-the-Water begged him to go his way, so he did.

At one place they met a man and his children driving along in a wagon. These people in the wagon were very poor. The father begged for something to eat. "Help me out," he pleaded. "My children are starving." Child-of-the-Water found a quarter. He threw it in the ditch and it turned into a great deal of money. Those people were loading the money into the wagon when Child-of-the-Water and the other man went on their way.

These two men went to the next town. The man still didn't know that he was with Child-of-the-Water. When they neared the place Child-of-the-Water handed him some money and said, "I have a little money left. Take this, go to town, and buy a chicken for us to eat."

The man went on and bought a roasted chicken. On the way back he got hungry and ate one of the legs. When he came to Child-of-the-Water he handed him the chicken.

"Where's the other leg?" he was asked.

"Oh, in this place the chickens have only one leg," the man answered.

Child-of-the-Water said nothing. They ate and went on. They came to the next town. There they entered a store. Child-of-the-Water asked the storekeeper for something to eat. The storekeeper looked at his dirty clothes and said, "Can you pay for what you want?"

"I have no money," Child-of-the-Water told him, "but I can do anything for you that you want."

"Then make my mother a young girl again. If you do that I'll give you a big pile of money."

"No, I don't want that."

"I'll give you this store."

"No, if I succeed I want just a little money. Now you must haul two loads of wood outside of town."

They did so. Child-of-the-Water had the wood stacked up. He had the old woman sitting on top. Then he set fire to the wood. The whole thing and the woman too, burned down to ashes. The next morning a big crowd came. "Bring two white sheets and spread them," Child-of-the-Water told them. He took some ashes from four places in the heap of ashes and put them on one of the sheets. He covered this sheet with the other one. Then he pulled the top sheet away. The mother of the storekeeper was there, and she was a young girl again.

They started on the road again. But the man wanted to get rid of Child-of-the-Water and acted cranky on purpose. Finally he told him, "You go on alone; I'm not going any farther."

Child-of-the-Water went on alone. The other man went back to town. The reason he had wanted to get rid of Child-of-the-Water was so he could try to do the same thing that Child-of-the-Water had done.

He went in a store and said just what Child-of-the-Water had said to the other storekeeper. The man who ran the place promised him a great deal of money and the store if he would make his mother young again. So he did everything Child-of-the-Water had done. He had wood hauled. He put the old woman on the pile. He made the fire. The next day he put sheets there and placed the ashes between them. Then he lifted the top sheet, but instead of a young woman, nothing but ashes was there. They put him in jail for life for it.

Child-of-the-Water came back to this town. He walked past the jail where this man was held. The man called to him, but at first Child-of-the-Water made believe he did not hear and passed him by. Then he came back and said to the man, "How did you get there?"

"I tried to do the same thing you did, and it wouldn't work."

"Ask the man to give you another chance."

So the prisoner asked for another chance and was given it. This time Child-of-the-Water went with him and helped him. They did as before with the ashes, putting them between the sheets, but this time, when the top cover was pulled away, the young woman was really there. So the man was freed.

### 6. *The Departure of Child-of-the-Water*[1]

Each group was placed in the world. Child-of-the-Water told the Indians to increase. They were living by a river. The children were swimming and having a good time. The chief had six sons. Child-of-the-Water came over and made himself a homeless boy. The children made fun of him. The chief bade them stop because he couldn't help it.

The six brothers took Child-of-the-Water and they sat under the shade of a tree and questioned him. Child-of-the-Water answered that he would not tell where he came from.

The eldest boy said, "Let's all go home." He told Child-of-the-Water he would give him clothes. Child-of-the-Water said, "No." Each

---

[1] This is obviously the Christian account of the death and resurrection of Jesus, who is now identified by the Apache with Child-of-the-Water.

time they ate he said he had eaten. But they dressed him and he was a nice looking young man.

Child-of-the-Water said, "Brother, I am going to be with you only thirty-one days." All this time the boys counted the days and wondered who he was. They got to love each other.

There was a hill in the east. At the end of the thirty-one days Child-of-the-Water said, "Let's walk there." The other five cried after him, but Child-of-the-Water said, "I am going home from there." So just the eldest boy and Child-of-the-Water went on. When they arrived they looked over the country where they had been. Then Child-of-the-Water said, "Look over there. It is good country."

When the boy looked back Child-of-the-Water was gone. He looked all over for the hiding place. Then Child-of-the-Water came through the sky on a cloud and said, "Brother, what are you looking for?" The boy stood looking up with tears in his eyes. Child-of-the-Water thought that the tears were at seeing him go above. The boy thought something would happen to him. Then Child-of-the-Water said, "The next time I return we will go back together, as I am lonesome for you."

Before Child-of-the-Water left he had told the boy he was returning to his mother's birthplace. Child-of-the-Water appeared to the people there. There the people killed Child-of-the-Water. He had the power to do as he pleased but said he would rather die and fix a place for the Indians. After he was dead he was put in a cave with a big stone. He had a big wound of a spear on his left side. Somebody said, "If there is room for four fingers in the wound, it is he." And it was he, dead.

His mother, White-Painted Woman, was sitting outside crying. Two days later a voice from within said, "Mother, don't cry. We will see each other again." So she left. On the third day the mother returned. No one was in the cave. A voice in the sky said, "I am up here now."

He told his mother and the others that he was returning to his father. "I have done all I could, so I am returning. But watch for me, as I am returning to you with everlasting life."

The biggest thunder on earth was called his father.

## C. Stories of the Giant

### 1. *Two Women Play Dead and Escape from the Giant*[1]

The giant used to kill people. There were two women hunting for wild berries. The giant came along. They saw that they couldn't get away. But they knew that he wouldn't eat anything dead that he had not killed himself, so they took off their clothes and played dead. Giant came along and saw them. He took a stick and poked their nipples. He played for a while and then got tired and left them. When he was gone they got up and ran away.

[1] According to one informant stories of the giant should be told only at night.

## 2. *Horned Toad Saves a Woman and a Boy from the Giant*[1]

The giant caught a woman and a little boy when they were out picking berries. He put them in his basket. While he was carrying them, they defecated in the basket. Then, as they went under a tree, they caught on to a limb and got out.

Giant got tired and put the basket down. He saw that they were gone and saw the excrement there. He looked back and saw them coming down from the tree. He started after them. They ran and cried, but he was gaining on them.

But as they ran they saw a horned toad. "Pick me up," he called to them. "The giant is afraid of me."

They stopped and picked up the horned toad and held it up. Sure enough, the giant was afraid and ran and they were saved.

[1] The Mescalero have elaborated these same themes. Similar tales are told about Big Owl by the Lipan (Opler, *Myths and Tales of the Lipan Apache Indians*, p. 60) and also by the Jicarilla (Opler, *Myths and Tales of the Jicarilla Apache Indians*, p. 74). For the last two tribes, Big Owl has much the same attributes as, and is the functional equivalent of, Giant among the Chiricahua and Mescalero.

## II. THE CONTEST FOR DAYLIGHT

### A. THE MOCCASIN GAME

1(a). *The Moccasin Game for Day or Night*

I don't know whether this story should come before the story about Child-of-the-Water, but in that story it was already day and night. In the story I'm going to tell now it was always night. This story explains the origin of the moccasin game.[1] My father used to start the story like this: he would say, "This is how we got our daylight."

All the birds in the air and all the animals which are four-legged divided themselves into two groups. The birds were on one side and the animals were on the other. The birds got together. They said, "Let us have a game. It is always night and we do not like it. Let's have a game and play for day. Let's see if we can win daylight." So they agreed to it. All the birds were on one side, and the four-footed animals on the other. They were playing the moccasin game. They said, "We are betting our lives." So if the birds won, they were going to get daylight and begin killing the losers.

When all the birds were on one side and all the animals on the other, they made the four holes on either side. They did this near a big high bluff. This cliff was east of them. They were down in a hollow playing. Each of the holes counted a different amount. I have played the game, but I have forgotten it. I believe the highest score was ten. They have many sticks tied up in bundles. I don't remember how many each side

[1] The moccasin game is one of the most important Chiricahua games of chance. It is played in winter only (for the snake and the bear are not abroad then) and at night. If the game has not come to an end by daybreak, the contestants must blacken their faces with charcoal before continuing, for the first moccasin game was concluded by daybreak. Both sexes participate, sides are chosen, a fire is kindled on a level place, and each side buries on its side of the fire four moccasins in a row, with only the tops visible. A blanket is held up between the opposing sides, and, while his fellows are vigorously singing songs descriptive of the antics of the animals and the birds in the first game, a member of one group places the bone in one of the moccasins on his side of the fire. The blanket is then lowered and someone of the other side attempts to strike, with a stick usually, the moccasin in which the bone is hidden. Should he strike correctly, the bone passes to his side for concealment. Should he miss, his group must pay to the opposition a certain number of yucca counters, the number depending upon how many moccasins away from the correct one his guess was. When one side has won all of the limited number of counters, the game ends. There are a number of variations and special plays, such as the one described in footnote 2, p. 26. Individual wagers on each stroke of the stick are made and much property is wagered on the final outcome of the game.

The story of the moccasin game, too, can be told only at night and in winter. "If you tell this story in summer, you will see bad animals like the rattlesnake," an informant explained.

23

uses or how many there are in a bundle. The side winning all the sticks
was to begin killing the members of the losing side.

In those days there was a great monster, a giant. Giant was on the
animals' side.

They started playing. Pretty soon the birds were losing. You know
that the turkey now has three or four tendons in his leg. He didn't have
them before the game. Early in the game Turkey had put some of the
counters in his moccasin and had gone to sleep. He had told them to
wake him up if they were losing. Now the birds were losing all their
counters. Finally they had just one more counter. Coyote was so anxi-
ous to kill these birds that he was all ready to begin. So they woke up
the turkey. "Wake up, old man!" the birds cried. "We are losing, and
they are eager to kill us. You have a few more sticks in your moccasin.
Take them out and play." Turkey got up. Then he began to play.

"I've got a few counters here still," he said. And he went over there
and hit. Soon the birds had nearly all their counters back.

Then Turkey began to win sticks from the other side. He kept doing
it and doing it until the animals had just a few more counters.

Just before Turkey began to win from the animals, Coyote stood
in the middle and said, "I'm going to stay here and play with the win-
ners. I'm going to help the winning side."

The animals had just about two more sticks, and day began to break.
You know the wren, a little bird that goes on the cliffs. He went before
the animals, he was so happy, and sang:

"Daybreak is coming!
Daybreak is coming!"

This made the giant so angry that he took a stick from the fire and
pushed it right at Wren. "Keep still, there isn't going to be any daylight," he said as he jabbed the bird. That is why Wren has a black
mark on his head now.

Then the little wren flew up on the cliff on the east side, and just then
the cliff opened a little. There was a hole right beside the wren through
which daylight was coming. The wren sat right in the hole. "Daylight!
Daylight!" he was saying, he was so happy. Then the animals lost the
last stick, and the birds began killing them.

Just before the end of the game, when the animals had only about
two or three counters left, Giant said, "I'm too heavy; I can't walk very
fast. I'm going to leave now." Just then all the counters were lost, and
they began to kill all the animals.

The birds all got after the giant. They were shooting at him with
their little arrows, but they couldn't kill him. Lizard came along. He
had been with the animals, but he said, "I know where his heart is. Let
me help you kill him." So they did not kill the brown lizard, but gave
him a bow and arrow. He ran to the giant. "There's his heart, right under his hind foot," he said. This little lizard shot the giant right under
his hind foot and the monster fell.

Most of the other animals got away. They tried their best to kill the snake. They chased it to a big cliff, but it got in a crevice of the cliff where the arrows couldn't reach it.[1]

Then they got after the bear. Just a little way from the place where they were playing the game was a thicket. Bear went right in there and got away. Therefore if you want to look for bears, that is the place to find them, in the thickets. When the birds started shooting at the four-footed animals, the bear was in such a hurry to get away that he put his moccasins on the wrong feet. His feet are still that way today.

This place where they played is in Arizona. They call it Mescal Mountain.[2] It is a holy mountain. I have never been there. My father has told me this story many times. About 1885 my father saw this place where the game was played. Everything there is as fresh as if the game had been played yesterday, though it happened hundreds of years ago. The holes are as fresh as if they were made this morning. The fire place is still there. You can see where they shot arrows. The arrow is sticking in the cliff where the snake went in. The big hole is there in the cliff to the east where the morning light came through. At the place where they killed the giant and he fell over four hills there are white rocks that were his bones. You can see the thicket where the bear went. Chatto says that he knows the place.[3] There are mountain ridges that run east of San Carlos, Arizona. If you follow these you come to a high mountain. It is a holy mountain. The nearest town to this place that I know of is Duncan, Arizona. The mountains at Duncan lead to the place where the game was played.

I asked the Navaho about this, and he said it was true.[4] He knows the story almost the same way. The Navaho get power from that place too.

### 1(b). *The Moccasin Game for Day or Night (Variant)*

At the time of the moccasin game there was no sun, no light; nothing but darkness all the time. All kinds of birds with wings and all kinds of four-legged animals were talking against each other just as these Indians do now. So the main bird and the main animal (I don't know which they were) said, "We don't like each other's ways. Let's play a moccasin game and the side that wins will kill all those on the other side."

At the same time something told them, "If you beasts and birds are going to play, when one side wins it will be daybreak; light will come through the mountains. No matter which side wins, at that time it will be daybreak through the mountain."

[1] This is supposed to explain why the snake, though it was on the side of the evil ones, exists today. The next passage explains the persistence of the bear, which the Chiricahua consider a most dangerous and evil animal.

[2] The informant identified this as the Mogollon Mountains.

[3] Chatto was a well-known Chiricahua whose activities as a scout in the Geronimo campaign of 1886 brought him into prominence. He has recently died.

[4] A Navaho who was visiting the Mescalero Reservation at the time this tale was recorded.

All the birds with wings were on one side and all the four-legged animals on the other. They made one hundred and fifty strips of narrow yucca.[1] Four of these were long and counted ten each and one was tied at the middle and counted four. The side which is hitting holds the bundle in this game. If they lose they give out what they have lost. When the other side is hitting, the bundle is passed to them. When all the strips are gone from the bundle they play for each other's strips until one side has them all.

Coyote was there. He was a smart one. When he would see that one side was winning, he would go on that side. He kept changing sides.

About midnight they were playing pretty hard. Gopher was on the four-legged animals' side. When they had the bone he burrowed down there and watched. When the birds hit correctly he took it and hid it in another moccasin.

All the insects with wings were on the birds' side. All the four-legged creatures, even Lizard, were on the animals' side.

At first the birds nearly got beaten. Then Road-runner got the stick. He hit the right one and got the bone out. The birds won back a few and then they lost the bone. But Road-runner got it again and the birds made more. Road-runner never missed. Because of this, one of the animals got angry and poked him with a fire stick. That's why he has red on his face now.

After a while the birds had most of the sticks. The animals had only three or four counters left. The birds had the bone, the animals were hitting. The animal who was to hit asked, "Can I have *ke'ešči?*"[2] The birds said, "All right." Then the animals won the bone back and they continued and got half of the sticks back too. The score went back and forth. They shouted and sang, and sang pretty songs too. The birds were losing now. So Turkey stole a few sticks. That's the way they do here still. Turkey put them in his moccasin and he has them there still. When you kill a turkey you see them.

The birds were gaining again and now the animals were losing heavily. Both sides played hard for their lives and the daybreak. The animals kept on losing the counters. They had only four or five left. Then the giant, who was playing on their side, got up. He said, "We're going to lose our lives. I can't go fast, so I'll go ahead." He had big testicles and couldn't go fast. He started off slowly but he got tired and lay under some cholla. He put his testicles up and sat under them, using them for a shade.[3]

Then the animals lost their last sticks, and just then daylight came

---

[1] The usual number of counters described for the game is sixty-eight, of which four count ten and the others one each.

[2] *Ke'ešči* is a manner of playing in which the striker attempts to avoid rather than to hit the moccasin in which the bone is hidden. The literal meaning of the word is "moccasin empty."

[3] The ponderous gait and large testicles of Giant are among the traits characteristically associated with him.

through the mountain. Since that time we have had daylight. At the morning of the moccasin game a big hole appeared in the mountain; this hole wasn't there before. It is still that way. The birds won the light at that time.

As soon as they won, the birds took the arrows and spears and killed many animals. Those which were killed then are not living on the earth now. Those living today are the ones that were saved in the battle, the ones that got away. The coyote was on the birds' side when they won, so they didn't harm him.

They came to the giant. He tried to get his testicles off the bush but they wouldn't come. By the time he got them off, the birds were up to him. They shot him full of arrows, but he wouldn't fall. Then Lizard, though he was on the animals' side in the game, helped the birds. He said, "Give me a bow and arrows. I know where he keeps his heart."

They gave them to him and he went into the ground. As Giant came along he shot upwards and shot the giant under the foot. Giant cried, "That's where I keep my heart!" and fell.

The snake got away. They shot many arrows into him. But he got between some rocks and was safe. The birds stood shooting arrows into the crevice where he disappeared. Those arrows are still there. Paul and Sundayman saw the place before they died and told us.

They went after Bear. They were shooting at him and fighting with him near Deming, New Mexico. Just as they were getting the best of him he got into the thickets there and escaped. And there are many bears in that place today.[1]

[1] These variations and additions are summarized from versions not here included: Originally there was no night—only light. Badger was carrying something in a basket which he warned Coyote not to untie. Coyote disobeyed and let out night. It was then night all the time. During this period of darkness the animals and birds could speak like humans and all spoke the same language. The small and harmless animals as well as the birds wanted daylight; therefore Gopher was on the side of the birds and aided that side by tunneling under the moccasins and moving the bone when the opposite side had struck correctly. Road-runner hid counters in his moccasins and was struck in the face with a firebrand. Giant (identified as Big Owl by one informant, which is interesting in view of the Big Owl stories of the Jicarilla and Lipan) could not be slain because of his armor of flint. Crow (this from one informant only and seems atypical) advised that he be shot under the foot. Giant fell over four ridges. Hawk and Buzzard chased the bear into a thicket. He escaped by changing into two, three, and finally four bears when they began shooting. Snake was beaten on the rocks and much of his body was severed. He escaped and survives today because he allowed his eyes to fall into a rock crevice. His opponents tried to shoot arrows into the crevice but could not reach the eyes. When the birds and animals left the site of the game each was speaking a separate language.

In the story of the game for night or day each animal and bird has a song which reminds one of his character and of what he did in the game. The moccasin game songs should not be sung in the summertime when the snakes are out, or a snake will bite one. The game is played in late fall and winter only. The story of the first moccasin game should not be told during the day.

# III. THE COYOTE CYCLE AND OTHER ANIMAL, BIRD, AND INSECT TALES

## A. THE ORIGIN OF DEATH

### 1. *Coyote Causes Death*

Raven said that he didn't want death in this world. "I'll throw a stick in the river. If it sinks there is going to be death, but if not, everything will be all right," he said.

Then Coyote came along and said, "I'll throw a rock in the river. If it sinks people will die. If it doesn't sink there will be no death."

Raven threw the sticks and they floated off. Then Coyote threw the rock and it sank.[1] After that people began to die off.

## B. THE COYOTE CYCLE

### 1. *Coyote's Enemy Sends Him Away on Rising Rock and Steals His Wife*[2]

After the gambling for day or night, the coyotes moved out and traveled to the place where the rising rock was.[3] The coyotes were camping

[1] This is a reversal of the Jicarilla story, in which Raven and not Coyote is responsible for death. (Cf. Opler, *Myths and Tales of the Jicarilla Apache Indians*, pp. 44–47.) In the Lipan account also it is Raven who is charged with the introduction of death.

[2] A second version, combining stories 1 and 2 of this cycle, deviates in the following particulars: Coyote is living with the family of another man. In order to possess this man's wife, he sends her husband up on a rock during a hunt. He then tells the woman that her husband is lost and they might as well live together. Meanwhile Old Woman Bat brings the husband down in a basket secured by one strand of spider's web. Coyote has just obtained a promise from the woman that she will come to him later that night when the husband is heard approaching. Coyote jumps from the woman to his old place behind the fire. As the husband comes in he greets him and says, "See, I am taking good care of your wife just as I used to."

A third variant, also combining Coyote stories 1 and 2, shows the following differences: Coyote is on his way to visit a family when he meets its head and sends him up on the rock. He marries the man's wife and abuses his son, addressing him as "Son of the man who went up on the rock" and forcing him to carry in meat from the hunt. When the man arrives home Coyote jumps to the other side of the fire and pretends he is tending it. The husband forces Coyote to heat four rocks, wrap tallow around them, and swallow them, telling him that if he accomplishes this he may keep the woman for his wife. As he swallows the fourth hot rock, Coyote dies. For a recurrence of the rock swallowing theme see p. 63.

[3] They usually begin the Coyote story with the one of the rock that went up in the air. But I have heard it other ways too. Different tribes and people have made it different. But my father always started with the story about the rock. Some begin with any story now. There is no Indian living who could tell them all from the beginning. The government kept the Indians pretty busy and for a long time they had no chance to start the stories and go right through. (Inf.)

28

right around close to this rock. And in that camp there was one coyote who had a pretty wife and a little boy.

Every now and then these coyotes would go to the rock. One would say to another, "You get on that rock over there." And then some of those coyotes would say, "Rock, rise up with that man." Then the rock would start to go up, far up toward the sky. Then they would tell that rock, "Come down with that man again." So that rock would bring that fellow down again.

One time this coyote who had the pretty wife happened to be among the crowd. Another coyote who had it in for him was standing in the crowd also. And he told the coyote who had the pretty wife to get on that rock. Coyote got on the rock. And the fellow who had it in for him said, "Rock, go up with him." And it began to go up with him. Then at the command, "Come down again, Rock," it came down with the coyote. And that coyote with the pretty wife said, "This is a very fine thing! I'd like to go up again." So he was sent up and down until the fourth time. Then his enemy told the rock to get up out of sight and to stay that way. The rock did so. And all the camp was going on a journey, moving. And Coyote was up there out of sight and couldn't get down.

Every day the coyotes were moving farther away.

As soon as that coyote got out of sight on the rock, the other coyote got his wife. He married that woman and abused that little boy. Every time he brought meat he took the muscle meat, the toughest part that isn't worth eating, and he threw it to the boy. He would say, "Eat that, you! Your father went up on a rock, he went up in the sky." And he would say, "Your father is dead. Your father went up on a rock into the sky." He was mean to him. He told him that every day.

Now we go back to the boy's father. He was up there on the rock. And he saw some bats playing around above him. Coyote called to them, "Hey, you folks up there playing with your children, come down here! I want to see you."

And one of the children said, "Wait! Someone's saying something down below."

And Coyote yelled the same thing again.

Then they heard him and went down there. And he began to beg help from those bats. He said to one of them, "Old man, won't you please carry me down?"

The bat told him, "We might fall."

But he kept begging him, "Carry me down."

So the bat went away and got a basket. And it was fastened across his head and hanging on his back. He came back. The first thing the coyote did was to look over this basket and the strings to see how strong it was. The bat had a thin string, just a hair, as a rope for that basket.[1]

[1] For a similar motif see p. 99. Note that the bat in this story is a male. Usually Old Woman Bat acts in this capacity.

Coyote said, "What kind of string is that? That's going to break with me; then I will fall."

The bat answered, "This will never break."

Coyote said, "All right, let's see you put four big rocks in it and jump around with it here." So Bat put four rocks in and did what the coyote asked him to do. It didn't break. Then Coyote said, "That will be all right."

The bat, before Coyote got in the basket, told him, "I'm going to tell you just one thing you must do: shut your eyes after you get in the basket and keep them shut all the way down. If you ever open your eyes, we're going to fall and break our legs.

Coyote said, "All right."

So they started going down to the ground. When the bat started he said, "Rock, stick, stick, stick." He just kept saying that all the way down until he was just a little way from the ground.

Then Coyote began to yell, "I just have to look!"

Bat said, "Don't you do it, for then we're going to fall."

Coyote insisted, "I just have to open my eyes."

Bat begged him not to. But the coyote looked and they fell, and the bat hurt his shin. But they were down, and the coyote went on his journey.

## 2. *Coyote Seeks His Family and Kills His Rival*

Coyote started out just as fast as he could to follow the people who were traveling, his people. They were several days ahead of him.

He got back where his camp was before he went up on that rock. He asked the fire poker, "How many days ago did they leave?"

It said, "Ten days ago."

He went to the next place where they had stopped. He asked the ashes how long ago they had left. Ashes told him they had gone nine days before. He went to the next place and he asked an old brush bed how many days ago they had been there, and it told him eight days. He went to the next place and asked the horse ribs used for tanning hides[1] how many days ago they had been there, and he was told seven days. At the next place he asked the posts[2] used for tanning the hides, and they said six days. At the next place he found a bone that had been chewed on and thrown away there. He asked the same question and was told five days. At the next place he asked a rock, and it told him they had left four days ago. At the next place he asked a wickiup pole,[3] and he was told they had left three days before. And all these things

[1] Horse ribs were used by the Chiricahua as tools for removing the hair from the hide.

[2] These are the "leaning posts" over which the hide is placed when the hair is removed.

[3] The wickiup or dome-shaped dwelling of brush was the ordinary house type of the Chiricahua, though the Eastern band made some use of the tipi on occasion.

told him the direction in which his people had gone. At the next place he asked a tree, and it told him the people had left two days before. He went to the next place where they had camped and asked a little bunch of grass. He asked everything that would talk to him and show him the way. The grass told him they had left one day before.

Next he asked a path. "You're almost to them," it told him. "Just follow me." And he found them.

He went to one camp and asked where his wife was camping. At that camp those people told him how his son was treated and who had his wife. And so he went to his wife's camp. No one, not even his wife, knew when he got there. And he went into an arrow quiver which was hanging inside. The man who had taken his wife was out after some meat.

After a while there came that man with some meat. And the woman's husband was in the quiver. His wife was cooking meat for the other coyote, and when his meat was cooked, he got the very best part of it. He threw the muscle, the part you could hardly chew, to Coyote's son and told that little fellow, "Eat that. Your father is dead, and a rock went up in the sky with him."

Just about that time Coyote was trying to get out of the quiver. The other coyote looked up and said, "What's the matter with the wind, shaking my quiver?"

Then the first coyote jumped out and took the bow and arrows out. He pulled the bow at once and shot that other coyote with several arrows and killed him right there.

And he told his wife, "Drag that coyote out! He stinks and is dirty! Go on and carry him out. Take him to that hollow over there."

While she was dragging the coyote out, she was crying. She didn't cry aloud so that her husband would know anything about it. But it showed in her eyes that she had been crying when she got back to camp.

Then her husband looked at her in a suspicious way and got after her. He said, "It looks as if you've been crying over there. Have you been crying?"

She said, "No, I was coming against the wind and something went in my eyes."[1]

### 3. *Coyote Marries His Own Daughter*

Coyote had a family; I don't know how many children he did have. The oldest daughter was a very pretty girl. Coyote and his family were in a camp in one place, and he was figuring out how he was going to get a chance to marry his own daughter. Finally he had it planned, the way he was going to work it.

He told his wife and children, "I've got lung trouble." But he wasn't sick. Nothing was wrong with him. He said, "This is a very contagious disease, and I don't want to spread it among my children. You see that

[1] For this same very human motif see p. 64.

tree over there. You make me a bed up in that tree and feed me, and
I'll stay there."

So right away his wife got busy and made that bed up there, and
when the bed was ready she told him.

He managed some way to get hold of a piece of spoiled liver, and one
time when they weren't looking he carried it up there.

Now he was up there on his bed. And his wife came under the tree
once in a while. Then he told his wife and children to sweep under the
tree very thoroughly. "Remember, I have a bad disease. If worms drop
on the ground, don't look for me.[1] You must all go away and leave me
up here." He told his wife to come every day and watch for those worms
to drop. That would mean he was dead, he said.

Before he dropped any worms he told his wife what to do. He said,
"If the worms happen to drop, that's a sign that I'm gone. Then you
can go your way with the children. Then the first man you meet who
has four reeds and is carrying four prairie-dogs must be given the oldest
girl." That's the advice he gave to his wife.

All his children and his wife knew that on the right side of his head
he had a big black wart.

Sure enough, one day the worms began to drop, and the woman came
and found them. She went back to her children and said, "The old man
is gone." They were crying. Right away they left the place.

Just as their home was almost out of sight, the smallest child looked
back over there by that tree and saw his father run off. He looked again
and saw his father trying to run ahead of them. The little boy said,
"Mother, wait!" They stopped. He said, "I saw my father jump off
that tree over there." But he was too small to be believed.

Before they had left the place, the mother had told the children not
to say, "My father." She had said, "Never call the dead. The ones that
are gone, never to come again, never call them." That's what the
mother had told the children just before they left. She said she would
slap the first one that did. So she slapped the little boy now. "I told you
not to say that," she said.

"But it was my father. I saw him jump off that tree and run over
there."

Then she whipped him. But that little coyote was right.

They went on their way. They all cut their hair. They were going
along there crying.[2]

Coyote had jumped off the tree and now he went and got those things
he had mentioned to his wife. He was all dressed up, and he went to
meet his family.

So there they came. He met them. The woman and children looked
very sad. He asked, "What is all this about?"

[1] Tuberculosis is thought by the Chiricahua to be caused by worms which
consume the lungs.

[2] The desertion of the place of death, the restriction against calling the name
of the dead, the hair cutting, and the wailing are all Chiricahua death customs.

The woman said, "The old man is dead. He told us when the worms dropped, we must leave. Now he's gone."

Coyote said, "Oh, my dear uncle! He's gone!" He began to cry.[1] Before he got through crying he said, "That man used to be wise. Perhaps he said something before he died?"

The woman answered, "Yes, he said something before he died."

Then Coyote was eager to know what it was he did say and asked the woman, "What did he say?"

She told him, " 'The first man that you meet carrying four of those reeds and four prairie-dogs must be given our oldest daughter.' That's what he said."

And he told that woman, "You see, I knew he must have said something before he died, he was so wise." He said, "You all go ahead and wait there for me. I'm going to see whether I can kill some rabbits or something for you."

And they camped there. He showed them the four reeds and the prairie-dogs he had and he married the girl.[2]

Then they got where they wanted to stop. They made their brush hut. Coyote already had his place, and his mother-in-law was nearby. He went to his camp. His wife was there with him. And he lay down with his head on his wife's lap on the sunny side of the camp. His wife was looking for lice. He had his head over to one side, hiding the wart. Every time she wanted to look on that side he would say, "The lice have gone on the other side."

The girl thought, "What's the matter that he won't let me feel on that side?"

Having someone go through your hair makes you sleepy. He almost fell asleep several times. Finally he went sound asleep. Then she turned his head a little and found that big wart. She knew it was her father. She quietly got away from him and went toward her mother's place.[3]

She cried, "It's he! It's he!" She said it several times, and he heard it and woke up.

He called, "What 'he'? What 'he'? Come back here, come back!"

She ran to her mother and said, "Mother, he's got a big wart on the side of his head. That's my father."

Her mother ran and got a big rock to drop on his head. Before she got to him he ran away.[4]

---

[1] A Chiricahua who sees a funeral party or a newly bereaved family may either avoid the encounter or "help wail for the deceased." To simply act as a curious bystander is considered an insult.

[2] Here the informant exclaimed, "That's just the way it is! Man does just like Coyote. Ever since Coyote did it, man does those things. He even marries his own daughter sometimes." Then followed the details of two alleged cases of father-daughter incest.

[3] The Chiricahua practice mother-in-law avoidance, and so Coyote's former wife had to have a separate dwelling.

[4] In the version collected by Hoijer (*op. cit.*, p. 27) Coyote's former wife kills him with this rock.

This was known already, that he had played that trick and married his own daughter. He went to two or three camps. Every time he came they would say, "That's the fellow that married his own daughter." Everybody seemed to know about it.

Coyote didn't like it. He went off and sat down and thought, "How do they all know? All the little bushes, the rocks, and trees are notified," he said. He was out there by himself. He went away from there and found just one camp. He went to it. He said, "I went to all the camps, and as I came through I heard of a man who married his own daughter." Then he went on.[1]

### 4. *Coyote Bites Rock Rabbit*

Coyote went on his journey. He was hungry. Somebody stuffed a rabbit with rocks and put it just where he was going to pass. It was right in the grass. As Coyote was trotting along, he saw that rabbit. He was trying to get just as close as he could to make one jump and get it. When he was just the right distance to rush at it full speed and bite it, he made a dash and grabbed it with his teeth. It surely hurt him!

He said, "Oh, my teeth!" Coyote sat there, and his teeth hurt.[2]

### 5. *Coyote Allows Real Rabbit to Escape*

Coyote went on his journey again, went along, trotting. He saw a real rabbit. That rabbit was sitting right beside the path where he was going.

He said, "I will not take any more time to look at rock rabbits," and he passed it. Then he looked back, and that rabbit ran.

Then Coyote began to curse himself. He said, "Coyote's son! Worthless Coyote! Never will have any sense! Could have eaten the fat rabbit and instead let it go!" He was angry at himself and very hungry.

### 6. *Rabbit Runs through a Hollow Log and Escapes from Coyote*

After Coyote ran into that rock rabbit and missed the real one, he went on along the road. He was hungry and tired. Every rabbit he saw got away from him. At last, there near the path, he saw a rabbit sitting in a bunch of grass. He had to pass near it.

So he told the rabbit, "Just lie still, old man. The enemy are right

---

[1] A second version differs in these details: Coyote instructs his wife to give his daughter to a man whose face is painted white and who carries four prairie-dogs. The daughter sees her father jump from the tree after his "death" and is rebuked by the mother for saying so. Coyote hides from the woman who was formerly his wife. He is discovered by a scar on one side of his head.

In a third version Coyote bids his wife give the daughter to the first prairie-dog they meet after his death. He changes himself to a prairie-dog but is exposed when a characteristic sore on his head is found.

[2] A variant offers these details: Coyote catches and eats a rabbit. He throws the hide away. Another rabbit finds this, fills it with sand and stones, and sets it under a yucca bush in order to fool Coyote.

upon us! I'm lying still here. Be quiet!" And he kept going closer and closer. And before he knew it, the rabbit, who was scared and keeping still, was caught. Coyote had come up and grabbed him. So now he had caught one of them.

Coyote had that rabbit in his hands and was going along that path. He said, "There are four spots of red dirt just a little distance from one another here." He was telling that to Rabbit while he was carrying him. "Now I'm going to ask you a few questions before I eat you. I have been all over this country looking for you rabbits. I have looked in every bunch of grass very carefully, in the bushes, everywhere I think there is a rabbit. Now you tell me what sort of place you rabbits have been living in, for I couldn't find you all these times."

And the rabbit told him, "We live around here in the grass where you caught me, and we live around here on the plains, where you caught me. I don't know where you have been."

The coyote still didn't believe it. He said, "I've been everywhere and haven't seen you rabbits. You tell me where you rabbits are hiding and what kind of place you keep yourself in. You tell me the truth. We are coming to the last red spot of ground where I'm going to eat you."

"Well, don't hold me so tightly then. I can hardly speak the way you are holding me." That's what the rabbit told him. And the rabbit said, "Let me turn a little."

And the coyote loosened his hold a little, and the rabbit began twisting around. Before Coyote knew it, Rabbit had jumped out of his arms. Coyote got so excited he said, "Hey, there goes a rabbit!"

A little way from that place there was a bunch of trees and thick bushes. Rabbit ran toward the bushes, and Coyote was right after him. Rabbit came to a log. It had a hollow through it, from end to end. Rabbit ran into this hollow log and went right through it.

Then Coyote quickly pulled up some grass. He stuffed up one end so that Rabbit couldn't come back that way. Then he went around to the other end and stuffed it up. He thought that rabbit was in the hollow log, but it had gone right through. Then he went to some juniper trees and pulled off some branches. He threw them around the log. Then he set fire to that grass in the log and tried to burn out the rabbit. Rabbit was watching him from a distance and was laughing at him.

When those branches were popping, Coyote was talking to himself. He said, "Yes, there goes the eye, pop! It will be well done." And every time the fire popped, he said the head was bursting or that something was breaking. Soon the wind came and spread the fire, and he had all the country on fire. All the animals were suffering because of that fire.

### 7. *Walking Rock Chases Coyote*

Coyote met two other coyotes. Those two coyotes were standing near a great rock.

He asked those coyotes, "What is that rock?"

They said, "That is a living rock. It walks slowly, and it runs fast;
you can't outrun it. We've heard about you. You are a pretty bad
man. You'd better be careful about that rock. If you ever do anything
to this rock, it will surely run you down. You'd better be careful around
that rock."

But Coyote told the others, "Where did you ever hear of a rock that
runs! There is no such thing!"

So they said, "All right, go ahead and do what you want to about
it."

So he defecated on the rock. Then he started to walk away.

At once that rock rolled after him. He went a little faster. The rock
followed behind him. The faster he went, the faster the rock rolled. So
he talked to the rock. "Did you ever see my full speed?" he asked and
went off at full speed. He was fast all right, but the rock was a little
faster. It gained on him. Then he saw that running would do no good
and that he would have to apologize.

The rock made him clean it off. Then that rock rolled back to the
place where it came from.[1]

### 8. *Tip Beetle Listens to the Voices from Below and Escapes from Coyote*

Coyote went on his journey again. He was very hungry and he found
an insect, a tip beetle. The beetle was standing right on its head.

He walked up to the beetle. He told that beetle, "I'm the person
who eats nothing but fat."

The beetle still had his head down. He told the coyote, "Old man,
you let me alone. I'm listening to what they are saying down there
under the ground."

Coyote said, "Hurry and tell me, because as soon as you tell me what
they say I'm going to eat you." Pretty soon he said again, "Hurry up
and tell me what they say down there."

"All right," Beetle answered, "I'm going to tell you now what they
say down there. They are talking down under the ground, and they are
saying that they are going after a certain man who has been playing
some tricks back up here."

Then Coyote said, "I'm going over there; I forgot something. I'll
be back." But he was scared. He never came back. He went on his
journey.[2]

### 9. *Coyote Helps Lizard Hold Up the Sky*

Coyote went along again. And he came to an old tree, a tall one,

---

[1] According to a variant Coyote runs at length into a hole, which the rock covers. He promises to clean the rock and is allowed to come out.

[2] According to another version, Beetle gives as the message from below that
someone who has dirtied a rock along the road is to be caught and killed. Coyote,
who has committed such an act, leaves hastily to clean off the rock he has soiled.
When he returns the beetle is gone.

with all the limbs off, standing there like a post. He saw a lizard up
there, a fat brown lizard.

He stopped under there and looked at him. He said, "I'm a person
who eats nothing but fat. Come down here and let me eat you."

Lizard answered, "Old man, don't talk that way. The whole sky is
going to fall on us. I'm here because this tree is holding up the sky,
and I'm holding up the tree." Then Lizard said, "Catch on! Hold it!
I'm tired."

Coyote grabbed hold of the tree. The clouds were moving, and every
once in a while as he watched the sky it looked as if that post was falling.[1]

The lizard said, "You hold it while I go and get some fellows to
help us."

So he went off. Coyote was there alone. He was holding that tree
with all his might and main. Every once in a while he got scared and
looked up. He thought the sky was falling. He stood there all day and
was pretty nearly all in. He began looking for some hollow place to go
into before the sky should fall. He was nearly ready to run for it.

Finally he just jumped and ran to a hollow place. He lay there
frightened, looking up, and then ran as fast as he could to another
hollow place. He did this, going from hollow to hollow, until he got to
a bank, and he saw that the sky wasn't going to fall after all. Then he
went on his journey again.[2]

### 10. *Coyote Dances with the Prairie-Dogs*

Then Coyote went up into the mountains somewhere. He found an
old blue uniform coat where soldiers must have passed a long time ago
and lost it. So he came down on the flats where prairie-dog town was.
As he came to the town he was yelling.

He said, "You people see that big blue mountain over there. I had
a war with the soldiers all day and have killed all the enemy. Here is a
soldier's coat. What I want you people to do is to have a big dance
tonight to celebrate my victory."

And the prairie-dogs all notified each other and built a big fire that
night and they had a big dance.

Before they started to dance Coyote told them, "Honor me and sing
about what I have done for you. Sing of that mountain where I got
this coat and had that fight." And when they all started he told them,
"All right, have a good time."

He went out and found the hardest wood, a mulberry tree. He cut a
good-sized club and came back over there. After he got back with the
club he was running around there telling the prairie-dogs how to sing

[1] For another use of this element see footnote 2, p. 67.

[2] Another version relates that Lizard is on a stalk of yucca when approached
by Coyote. Lizard leaves Coyote holding the pole under the pretext of going to
get his children to help.

those songs. And one of these prairie-dogs, the chief I guess, had this coat on a stick, and they were dancing around it. He told them to sing the song this way:

"Far away over there a blue mountain juts out;
From there was brought this coat."

About midnight he told those prairie-dogs, "I have been in a big war all day, and I'm very tired. I'm going to take a nap. But have a good time anyway." And he went away.

While he made believe he was taking a nap, he went and filled up all the prairie-dogs' holes. He worked at this all night. And they were having a good time over there. Then he came back where those prairie-dogs were dancing. He had his big club.

He yelled, "That's the way to have a good time. Keep it up! I have killed all your enemies." And now he wanted to have his way about everything. He told them to stop for a moment and listen. He said, "All you fat prairie-dogs line up on this side, all the thin ones on the other. He strung them out just the way he wanted them. And he had that big club. Then he said, "Go ahead and have a good time."

They started dancing again. And he began dancing by himself, with that big club in his hands, around those fat prairie-dogs. While he was dancing he made a motion as though he was going to hit one.

"Oh, he nearly hit that fellow!" they said.

"No," Coyote told them, "can't you think? I'm just showing how I fought the soldiers."

But soon, sure enough, he started to club them; he knocked them right and left. He killed them until morning. He brought them to the fire; the fat ones on one side, the thin ones on the other. Then he lay down for a real nap.[1]

## 11. *Mountain-Lion Steals Coyote's Prairie-Dogs*

Coyote went to sleep all right. While he was sleeping there, Mountain-lion came around and took all those fat prairie-dogs and carried them off to the mountain. He took the very fattest ones and left the thin ones there.

Pretty soon Coyote woke up. At once he remembered that he had something cooking in the fire and was going to get plenty to eat. The first thing he said was, "It will be tender!" He walked over to the fire. When he got to the fire he saw the foot and tail of a prairie-dog sticking out. But it was a thin one. He said, "That's no good!" and threw it away. He kept pulling them out and throwing them in every direction.

---

[1] A second version indicates this difference: Coyote picks up old clothes at a place from which people have just moved away. He makes a pack of them, goes to a prairie-dog town, offers the garments as proof that he has killed many of the enemy, and promises to give away the clothes after a dance. Obviously this has reference to the practice of giving away booty at a victory dance.

Then he took a stick and poked around but couldn't find anything more in there.

He was very angry at himself for going to sleep. He said, "Coyote, son of Coyote, has no sense![1] Somebody got them all!" So he went around and gathered up what he had thrown away and ate those anyhow.

### 12. *Coyote Dives in the Water for Prairie-Dogs*

There must have been a river close by. Coyote had been throwing the prairie-dogs as far as he could before. After he ate those thin ones he went and lay down to drink in the water. One of those thin ones had landed in a tree over the river. Coyote saw its reflection in the water. He was sure that prairie-dog was right down in the water there. He was very sure and he wanted to eat it too. So he dove right down where he saw that prairie-dog.[2] He kept diving and couldn't find that prairie-dog in the water. He walked around on that bank and said, "It's right here." He dove and couldn't get it. His belly got full of water, and he was tired.

He lay down and saw that prairie-dog hanging on the tree. He said, "Coyote's son has no sense! Going through this country and has no sense!"

So he picked that prairie-dog off and ate it after all the hard work.

### 13. *Mountain-Lion and Coyote Change Each Other's Appearance*

Then Coyote went to hunt that mountain-lion. He said, "I'm going to fix you when I find you!"

When he found him, Mountain-lion was asleep. I don't know what kind of face he had before this, but Coyote pushed Mountain-lion's face in and shaped it like a cat's face.

When Mountain-lion woke up he noticed that his face was in the wrong shape. He said, "I wasn't this way before. What's the matter with my face?" Then he said, "That old fool, Coyote, must have been here. I'm going after him."

So the mountain-lion went down along the creek. He looked in the water first thing and saw how his face was changed, and he went along that stream and found the coyote sleeping. He said, "Right here I'm going to get even with you."

He shaped Coyote's face while he slept and pulled his nose and made it long. Then he went away.

Coyote woke up some time later, and he found that he had a long nose and a long face. It bothered him. He said, "I didn't use to be this way." He was angry with that mountain-lion. He said, "That old fool, Mountain-lion, must have been here changing me."

[1] One of the characteristic and mirth-provoking traits of Coyote is his abuse of himself when he has been deceived or mistaken.
[2] For a similar theme see p. 67.

He went down to the water and looked at his face and said, "My face didn't use to be this way."[1]

## 14. Rabbit Escapes from Coyote by Pretending He Is Not Alone

Coyote went along on his journey. And he saw a rabbit some distance away. He started after it. Just as he was about to catch that rabbit, it went into a log. It had a hole in there. Coyote got to that log and reached just as far as his arm could extend in the end where the rabbit was. He tried with all his might to pull that rabbit out. He could barely touch the rabbit with the tips of his fingers. Rabbit thought he was going to get pulled out of that hole almost any second. He was all alone in that hollow log. There was no other rabbit in there with him. That rabbit was trying his best to think of some way to escape from Coyote. Coyote was just about to pull him out, was just barely touching him by reaching as far as he could.

Suddenly the rabbit grabbed him right around the wrist, and that rabbit said, "Grandma, let me have the butcher knife! I want to cut his wrist off."

When the coyote heard what the rabbit said, he began to beg. He said, "Please, grandma, don't give him that butcher knife!"

Then the rabbit turned Coyote loose. He told him, "Go away now. Don't bother me."

## 15. Coyote Has Intercourse with His Mother-in-law

Coyote went on his journey again. He went where there were some other coyotes. He was a married man. He had a camp of his own, and his mother-in-law was camping near him. Of course, he didn't see her.[2]

One day he told his wife, "I'm going out hunting."

He went only a little way, to a brushy place near the camp, and saw a rabbit. He ran after that rabbit, but it went into a hollow log. He did everything he could. He crawled in there and tried to reach it, but he could barely touch it. Then he went to his camp and told his wife to ask her mother to try to get the rabbit. He said maybe her arm was longer than his. He showed his wife the log over there.

Coyote's mother-in-law went over there and his wife came back home. Coyote was making excuses to get away from the camp. He said, "I'm going over that way."

But he circled the bushes quickly just as his mother-in-law was crawling in that log. She was about half in, reaching for that rabbit. He ran over there as fast as he could and had intercourse with her. She didn't know how that happened or who did it.

[1] A similar tale in which two animals change each other's appearance is told by an Eastern Chiricahua informant of Coyote and Jack-rabbit. Jack-rabbit takes the place of other protagonists in Eastern Chiricahua Coyote tales often. He does not displace Coyote, however.

[2] Note the references to matrilocal residence and mother-in-law avoidance.

She looked for his tracks. She took a piece of stick and measured his footprint there on the ground very carefully. She took that stick home. Coyote was at home already, lying on his bed. He had his legs over the bed. He was stretched out, singing. He didn't want it to appear that he was the man who had done it.

Now the old woman called her daughter over to her camp. Coyote's wife went over there. The mother gave this stick to her. She told her daughter to go over there and measure Coyote's foot.

While he was happy and singing and pretending he hadn't done anything, his wife came in and, without saying a word, began to measure his foot in every way.

He looked up. He said, "What's the matter with you? What are you doing?"

His wife told him. She said, "While my mother was over there trying to get that rabbit, someone played a trick on her."

Then Coyote told his wife, "Don't talk like a witch![1] That's witch talk. Go away and don't bother me. You folks have witch mouths!"[2]

### 16. *Coyote Tries to Catch Turkey by Chopping Down Trees*[3]

Coyote went on his journey again. He saw a turkey in some pine trees. It was high up there in a tree. I don't know where he got the axe, but he got an axe, and he began to chop on that tree. Just about the time the tree started to fall, the turkey flew to another one.

Coyote went to that tree and tried to chop it down. He just kept doing that all day long until he was tired out. He kept chopping and Turkey kept flying to the next tree until Coyote was worn out.

### 17. *Coyote Follows Bumblebee's Instructions and Is Stung to Death*

Coyote went on again. He met a big bumblebee. The bumblebee had a little package. Coyote asked him, "Old man, what have you there?"

Bumblebee replied, "I want nobody to meddle with this; I want nobody to see it." That's what Bumblebee told him.

But anyway Coyote commenced to plead with him, "Old man, please let me see it anyhow."

"No," Bumblebee said, "I've heard that you're the wrong kind of fellow. I don't want you to see it. This thing is very valuable to me. I don't want you to know about it."

---

[1] Anyone who commits incest is considered a witch by the Chiricahua; anyone who dwells on the subject is likely to be suspect.

[2] These differences are found in a variant: Coyote, having designs on his mother-in-law, makes believe he is trying to get a rabbit out of a hole he knows is empty. He tells his wife to send her mother over, pleading that the older woman has a longer reach. He offers to stay behind a tree while she is getting the rabbit. After violating his mother-in-law, he leaves the region for good.

[3] For the use of the motif of this tale in another setting see footnote 2, p. 67.

But the coyote said, "Please let me see it anyhow."

And that bumblebee got tired of him and told him, "You can't see it here. You must take it home. Don't untie it until your wife and children have built you a little hut with cowhide over it and with a hole straight up in the middle at the top. Have them roll rocks up all around it and make it tight so you won't be able to get out. Go in there alone. Take off all your clothes and go in there naked. Now I've told you what to do. Be careful. Don't untie that bundle except in the hut."   ·

So Coyote received that little bundle. He was so eager to see what was in it that he began to run straight for home. And when he came within hearing of his camp he started yelling, "My wife, call all the children home. Hurry up! Make a little hut for me right now. Your husband's going to see something pretty!" That's what he said.

Right away they went to work building that little hut, just the way he described it. And they had hard work to roll up those stones. They left a little opening and then rolled rocks up to that, closing it when Coyote got in there. Just as he went in the hut Coyote told his wife, "Your husband's going to see something very pretty in here." And he went in there and said, "Roll those big rocks up and roll them close."

The bumblebee had told him just what to do. He had said, "You stand in the center of your hut and untie the package." Coyote was naked. He stood right in the center of that hut. His little house was made in such a way that he couldn't get out at all, and it would take some time to roll those rocks away and get to him, too.

Coyote began to untie the bundle. And when he untied it, he found that it contained about a thousand bumblebees that he had turned loose on himself. The bumblebees began to sting him. He was screaming in there; he was cursing.

"You dirty coyotes, you sons of Coyote, roll the rocks away and let me out!"

And those bees killed him and went out through the hole at the top and went back to their master, I guess.

### 18. *Coyote Visits Flicker; the Bungling Host*

Another coyote was taking a journey. This coyote went along. He came to a flicker's home. Flicker was sitting there. And Coyote came up to the flicker and sat down. For a while the coyote sat there, and the flicker threw his wings apart and made a noise the way that bird does. Coyote was afraid every time the flicker opened his wings and made a noise. Coyote said, "Oh!" every time and dodged.

So the flicker said, "Those are my wings; don't be afraid of them." But Coyote was afraid and dodged every time.

Then Coyote told Flicker, "Old man, you come and visit me some time soon."

So Coyote went home. He went to work and cut up the last cowhide he had to fit it on his arms, a piece on each side, like wings. He was preparing to have the flicker come to visit him. He tied the cowhide on and painted it red on the inside with red paint. And he sat down there with those wings, waiting for Flicker.

Finally here came that flicker. Flicker sat down over there, and Coyote was sitting over here with those cowhide wings. And every now and then he threw his arms up and tried to flap his wings. The flicker wasn't afraid of him at all, but Coyote told him, "Don't be afraid of the noise; it's just my wings."

Flicker went home and laughed at him and told his family, "I went to visit that old man, and he put a cowhide on for wings!"

### 19. *Coyote Tries to Lead His Family like Prairie Chicken and Kills Them*

Coyote went along and met Prairie Chicken. And Prairie Chicken had his family lined up in a row, one after another. Coyote met the head of the family. He said, "How pretty! Nice, so nice! Your children are strung out so beautifully, in line. How did you ever get them strung out that way?"

So that prairie chicken told him, "This is what I did to my family. I sharpened a good-sized stick, about three feet long and about as big around as a rope. And I took a rope long enough to reach every one of them. Then I lined them up. The mother was at the head of the line. And I sharpened this long stick and stuck it right through their hearts, and kept doing that, pulling the rope through each one. I did that to all of them, and that's how they are kept in line."

So right away Coyote started to run for home. When he came where he could be heard by calling, he yelled, "My wife, call all the children home. You're all going to look pretty. You're all going to be in line."

So the mother called all the children home. Coyote was sitting there, sharpening sticks just as sharp as he could. When he was ready he got his whole family lined up. Then he told them, "You're all going to be very pretty, and you're going to follow your mama."

Well, he stuck his wife first and pulled the rope through her breast so that she would be the leader. He went to the second quickly and did the same thing. He was working fast, not looking back to see what was happening, just thrusting the stick through and pulling that rope through them as fast as he could. The first ones began to stagger around, and when he got through with all of them he went to the first again, the leader. And he got hold of the rope and commenced to pull on it.

He said, "Get up! You shouldn't go to sleep so soon. You're all going to be very pretty. Get up!"

Then he found out that he had killed all of them. He had killed all his family. And he sat down there and wept. Then, wiping his tears away, he said to himself, "I'm a man! What's the use of crying?"[1]

---

[1] A variant relates essentially the same story of Coyote and Quail. At the first encounter Quail explains that he put the rope through the chests of the members

## 20. *Coyote Visits Deer; the Bungling Host*

Then Coyote went on. He came to a big deer. The deer had long horns. The deer moved his head from side to side. Coyote was scared. Every time the deer moved he dodged and cried, "Oh!"

The deer said to him, "These are my horns; don't be afraid."

The deer had a family. The deer said to his family, "We can't do much for the old man; go get that big round basket." And he began to sharpen some sticks about three feet long. He said, "The old man's hungry. We can't do anything but feed him." That's what that deer said. And he took that stick and told his family, "Bring that basket over here."

So they pounded up dry meat for him, put it in the basket, and pushed it over to him. Deer took the stick and shoved it up his nose. Then fat came out, and he mixed it with the dry meat. The deer gave this to Coyote and said, "Here, eat it. Don't take any of it home, not a bit of it." That's what he told the coyote.

But anyway Coyote stole some of the meat, slipped it away while he was eating. When he had had enough he told the deer, "Well, old man, you come over and visit my camp too some time."

So one day Deer came to Coyote's camp, and Coyote told his wife, "We can't do anything for the old man but feed him," and he began to whittle on a stick. He said, "Get me that basket." He wanted to do what Deer had done.

Before this Coyote had gone out and got some big brush and sticks and tied them on like horns. Now he acted like that deer. He began to shake his head back and forth. He said, "Old man, these are my horns; don't be afraid of them." But the deer was not afraid at all.

Then Coyote put in the basket some of the dry meat he had over there. That deer watched everything.

Deer told Coyote, "That's the same thing I gave you the other day."

But Coyote paid no attention. He put that basket before Deer, and in it was the same dry meat he had got from the deer. Then Coyote pushed the stick in his nose.

And Deer told the coyote's family, "Say, friends, if you expect to give me that meat, I don't want blood on it. He's going to get blood all over it. I won't eat it."

But anyway the coyote took this stick and thrust it in his nose. And right there he killed himself! Blood ran out of his nose and over all that meat.

The deer went home and told his family, "I went and visited the old man, and he killed himself!"[1]

---

of his family initially in order to train them, but that they no longer require this device.

[1] In a variant of this tale Deer shoots an arrow into the air and allows it to penetrate his side on its descent. The blood that spurts out he catches in the basket. Fat is obtained as already described and this food is cooked by his wife and

### 21. *Coyote Visits Goat; the Bungling Host*

Another coyote was going along. He met a goat family and visited them.

The goat told his family, "We can't do anything for this old man. The only thing we can do is to feed him."

They were on the side of a big bluff. Goat told his family to put a basket at the foot of the bluff. And while Coyote was watching, Goat got up on his hind legs and butted at that bluff with his head. And dry meat fell in the basket. Goat pushed it up to Coyote and said, "Go ahead and eat it. Don't take any of it home."

After Coyote had eaten, he hurried home. Before he went, he told the goat, "Old man, you come and visit me too."

When he got home he told his wife to move camp to a place under the bluff. She moved the camp. Then that goat came to visit him.

"Well," Coyote told his family, "we can't do anything for the old man. The only thing we can do is to feed him. Get that basket and put it by the big bluff over there."

The goat was watching everything that was going on. And Coyote got up on his hind legs and went with full force against that bluff. He cracked his head and killed himself.

So the goat went home and told his family, "I went and visited the old man, and he killed himself!"

### 22. *Coyote Carries Beaver Far from Water; Beaver Carries Coyote Far from Land*

Another coyote was going along the road. And he found a beaver sleeping on the bank of the river. He got under that beaver and carried him away from that river. He put the beaver down on the ground while he was still sleeping. Then he shook him and said, "Here, old man, wake up! I have never known you to live in this kind of country. Wake up!"

And that beaver woke up. He saw at once that there was no river, no creek, no water near. He was far from any water. So he began to beg Coyote, "Old man, won't you please take me to the river?"

Coyote said, "No, I'm not going to do it."

And the beaver said, "Please, old man, take me to the river."

Coyote replied, "No, I will not do it; my back is aching.[1] I'm not going to carry any beaver." That's what he said. And he went away. Beaver began to roll, roll, roll, and was pretty well battered up by the time he rolled back in that river. After that Beaver had it in for Coyote. He was searching for him along the banks of that river, wishing he would catch him asleep somewhere.

---

given to Coyote. This is not so far-fetched as it appears, for boiled deer's blood was eaten by the Chiricahua. When Coyote tries to emulate Deer he is killed by the arrow he shoots into the air.

[1] In a second version of this story it is explained that because Coyote complained of an aching back men are afflicted with that ailment today.

Finally Beaver did find that same coyote asleep on the bank of the river. Then Beaver got that coyote. He took him right into the river, swam with him. Out in the middle there was an island. He put Coyote there. Then Beaver said to him, "Old man, wake up! You're not used to living in a place like this!"

As soon as he woke up, Coyote saw water all around him. He couldn't swim. He said, "Old man, please, would you take me to the bank?"

The beaver said, "No, I will not."

But Coyote begged the beaver again. He said, "Please, old man, take me to the bank."

Beaver told him, "My back is aching. I don't carry coyotes."

The beaver dove and went away from him. And there Coyote stood on the island. He made a motion as though to go in the water, but he didn't dare go. He couldn't swim. After a while he made up his mind and jumped in the water. He floated down the stream and had a hard time, and he was almost dead when he got to the shore.

### 23. *Coyote Visits Bumblebee; the Bungling Host*

Coyote went and visited Bumblebee. Bumblebee had a little camp in a yucca stalk.[1]

Bumblebee told his family, "We can't do anything for this old man; the only thing we can do is to feed him." So they called Coyote in. And Bumblebee said to his family, "Get one of these stalks and shake it."

They had something lying under the stalk. When they shook the stalk many things to eat fell out.

Bumblebee said to Coyote, "Go ahead, help yourself. But don't take any of it home."

Anyway Coyote slipped some away. He took it home with him, and before he went home he said to the bumblebee, "Old man, come and visit me."

As soon as he got home he told his family, "You make a yucca stalk camp."

And they made that camp. Coyote stuck the things he had taken from Bumblebee on the stalk. The food was very sticky and dirty by this time, and it stayed there. He was preparing for the visit of the bumblebee. He went with his family into that camp, and now came the bumblebee visiting.

Coyote told his wife, "Spread something all over the ground around this place. The only thing to do is to feed that old man; that's all we can do. Shake the camp and feed him." He had that food plastered on the stalk. They shook the camp and just two or three things fell out.

---

[1] From an Eastern Chiricahua (Warm Springs) informant a variant was obtained which describes Bee's home as consisting of a number of yucca stalks resting together like a tipi. It is noteworthy that the Eastern Chiricahua, the band most influenced by the Mescalero and the Plains Indians, were the only members of this tribe to make any use of the tipi.

The bumblebee looked at what had fallen out and told Coyote, "That's the very food I gave you the other day, and it's very dirty!" And Bumblebee went away.

### 24. *Coyote Visits Prairie-Dog; the Bungling Host*

Coyote went to a prairie-dog camp.

Prairie-dog said, "I can't do anything else for the old man but feed him." So he began to whittle on four arrow shafts without any feathers on, and then he told his wife to build a fire and make coals while he was whittling on the arrows. Coyote was sitting right beside him. Prairie-dog put those four arrows in the coals. When those arrows got red, he pulled them out, and there came out very fat prairie-dogs, well cooked. And Prairie-dog said to Coyote, "Go ahead, eat some."

Coyote ate, then he said, "Old man, you come and visit me too."

So the prairie-dog did come and visit him.

Coyote told his wife, "Well, we can't do anything for the old man except to feed him. Build a fire." And he began to whittle on four arrows too. He put his arrows in the ashes just the way that prairie-dog had done. And he burned up all his arrows. Nothing else happened.

### 25. *Coyote Herds Goats and Uses His Employer's Wives, Makes His Pursuers Drunk with Mountain-Laurel Berries, Cuts Their Hair, and Sends Many Coyotes after Them*

Coyote went along again. This was another coyote. He went to a white man who was herding goats. This white man had two pretty wives, young girls,[1] and his home was a little way from where he was herding goats.

Coyote said to this man, "What pretty animals you are herding! Can I herd them?"

The white man said, "No, I've heard you're a pretty bad fellow. I like my goats.[2] I don't want anybody to herd for me."

But Coyote begged, "Old man, do let me herd them for you. I'd love to herd them for you." After a while he was allowed to herd them.

Then the owner of the goats said, "See that puddle of mud over there You herd them around, but don't let them go in that mud. It's pretty bad."

So Coyote said, "All right, all right, I'll do it that way."

Then the white man went back to his home. And Coyote drove those goats around and killed most of them. He cut off their heads and tails and stuck these in the mud. Then he ate some of the goats himself.

Then he went toward the house a little way and stood before the mud hole. He called to his master just as loudly as he could and told

---

[1] The Chiricahua permitted polygamy and are here attributing their usage in this respect to the white man as well. A second version also credits the white man with two wives, but a third variant mentions but one.

[2] In two other versions the animals are sheep.

him, "The goats have all got in the mud! They are stuck in the mud!" Then that white man came running.[1]

Coyote told him, "I think we ought to have a shovel for that hole." The white man agreed right away and told him, "You run over there and tell my wives to give you the shovel."

So Coyote started at once for the shovel. He went to the white man's house and said, "Your husband sent me over here to have intercourse with both of you."

"Our husband loves us so much he wouldn't tell you any such thing!" The man's wives told Coyote that.

"Well, if you don't believe it, step outdoors and I'll call to him and ask him." So he yelled at that white man, "These girls won't do what you say."[2]

The white man said, "Hurry up! Hurry up!"

And those girls were standing at the door and Coyote said, "You heard that, didn't you? 'Hurry up!'"

"Well, all right," they said. And he went in there and had intercourse with both of them.

Coyote got away. The white man came over. He said, "Where is that fellow? I sent him over to get the shovel."

They answered, "You sent him over here and he had intercourse with us; that's what you told him to do." And Coyote had gone away.

"Well," the white man said, "get ready. Let's go look for him." So they went quite a long way looking for him.

Meanwhile the same coyote made a circle and met those people again. He said, "Where are you folks going?"

They said, "We are looking for a fellow just like you."

So Coyote said, "I was coming along here, but I didn't see anybody. All coyotes look alike. I don't know what fellow you're looking for. But if you mean to find him, I'll make some medicine for you."

Then he went and got some red mountain-laurel berries and pounded them up and put them in water.[3] Those people drank it. (They say this surely makes you drunk! Mountain-laurel grows in Mexico.) Then, while the people were out of their minds, Coyote cut their hair in patches the way the Chiricahua cut their hair.[4] So there they were, crazy.

And Coyote went on; he left them there. He went to a big encampment of coyotes. When he came within shouting distance, he yelled, "There are people with their hair cut around their heads over here, a whole bunch of them."

[1] At this point in another version Coyote pulls at one of the tails he has stuck in the mud and it comes out.

[2] In another version Coyote shouts, "They won't give it to me." The man replies, "Give it to him at once! Do you hear!"

[3] The narcotic properties of mountain-laurel berries are well known. See Weston La Barre, *The Peyote Cult*, p. 105.

[4] The reference is probably to a minor rite of the Chiricahua held in the spring during which the hair of young children is closely cropped, except for patches which are left at certain places.

The children were very noisy playing around those camps. But right away the people told the children to stop and listen. They said, "We heard someone yell over there."

Coyote called out again, "There are people over here, a whole group of them, with their hair cut around their heads."

And the whole camp said, "Let's see what this is."

They all went to their horses. Dust flew so you couldn't see. Coyote was right in the bunch there. And it was so dusty! Some of them passed him with their horses. Another was passing and said, "Get behind me. Where is the place?"

Coyote refused to ride behind that fellow. He said, "I can get there faster this way." And he told him, "They are right over there near that little hill."

It was so dusty you could hardly see anybody. And Coyote got away from there. All these people came to the place where those white people were. They were completely crazy and were crawling around.

### 26. *Coyote Sells the Money Tree*

Coyote went along again. He had two or three dollars with him. There came some white people, prospectors or something; I don't know what they were. They had several pack mules, plenty of provisions, clothes, blankets, and their own saddle horses and saddles, good ones. And this coyote was sitting under a tree right by the path. Before these people came through he had put his few dollars on the limbs of a tree.[1] These white people came up to him. The tree was right by the path. He was sitting under it.

And these white people asked him, "What are you doing here?"

He said, "I'm watching my tree very closely here all day long."

They asked him, "What's on that tree?"

He said, "The tree is very, very valuable. This is the only tree that money grows on. There is no other tree like it anywhere."[2]

They said, "What do you have to do?"

"When I shake the tree I get all the money I want. It drops down."

"Well!" they said. "Suppose we buy that tree from you."

He told them, "You can't give me enough for it."

They said, "We'll give you everything we have. We will just get off. You can have the pack horses, the blankets, everything. We will just get off and sit under that tree the way you do. You take everything."

Coyote hesitated a little as if he didn't want to do it. Then he said,

---

[1] According to one account Coyote sweeps under the tree before he takes his place.

[2] In one version Coyote explains that money ripens on the tree every two or three months. In another account he says that the tree bears an annual crop of money, and it is claimed that the buyer still sits there every year waiting for the money to come.

"If I'm going to trade with you there's just one thing you must do. And if I'm going to trade with you at all, you've got to do just as I say." He said, "You men see those big blue mountains over there. When you see me go over that mountain with these horses and mules then you can shake the tree. Then you will have all the money you want. But if you shake the tree before I get over that mountain you're going to spoil the whole thing. You won't get much money."

One of these men said to him, "Let's see you shake the tree to see if any money is going to fall."

So Coyote shook the tree just a little. Sure enough a few dollars fell.[1] Maybe he left a few dollars there. Then they thought, "Sure enough, it bears money!"

So the men got off and sat under the tree, and Coyote shook hands with them. Then Coyote went behind all those horses and mules and began to drive them off. They watched him, and when he went over that hill, these fellows began shaking the tree, and about two dollars fell. And then nothing more would fall. They sat there all day, and this coyote was already in another big camp of coyotes over that hill where he had gone. At that camp he gave away all the horses, scattered them all over.

These men were watching the tree for several days. They were thirsty and hungry. I think some of them died of starvation. And those who were still alive decided to find that coyote. They went in the direction he had gone over the mountain.

They found a big camp and saw many coyotes scattered all over. It just happened that the right coyote met them at that camp; he was the first one they saw. The coyote asked them, "Where are all you men going?"[2]

And those men told him, "We came over here to look for a fellow."

"Well," Coyote said, "I'm just going along here. There are many people here. All coyotes look alike. I don't know which coyote you are looking for."

So these men went around here and there asking coyotes about the one who had tricked them.

And the guilty coyote had told these men, "There was a man here who brought in horses and saddles. But he has given them all away, and he went that way a while ago."

But the story reached Coyote that somehow or other they were on his trail, so he left the country and got away to other places.

---

[1] One account has it that Coyote agrees to shake the tree to prove his contention if what comes down is given to him.

[2] According to one version Coyote eludes his pursuers by putting on old clothes and making believe he is a poor man looking for work. He sends them in the opposite direction by claiming to have seen someone traveling that way with several horses.

### 27. *Coyote Sells the Bird under the Hat*

This coyote was going along after selling the tree. He sat down by the side of the road. He saw some prospectors riding along with good mules and horses. Right away he thought of something. He defecated right by the side of the road. He found a big hat and put it over his feces and sat there holding the hat as these fellows were coming.

Those white men asked him, "What are you doing here, old man?" He said, "I have a very large bird under this hat. It's a wonderful bird." He told them, "It's worth a fortune!"[1]

Those fellows said, "Well, old man, can you let us see it?"

And he told them, "No. I'll sell you the bird, but you must give me everything you have."

These men wanted to see what they were buying and kept asking to see it. But after a while they decided to give everything they had, to get off their horses and let the coyote take everything.

And Coyote told them just what to do. He told them, "Don't move the hat until I get over that ridge.[2] Then you can get around and each get your hand ready and lift the hat a little and catch the bird, because if it gets away from you now, you never will get it, for that bird comes back to me no matter where I am."

He gave them all this advice, and they were holding down the hat as he had told them; and he went away, driving all the horses and mules just as fast as he could go.

They watched that coyote get over the mountain. Then they began to get ready, going around that hat and getting ready to lift it. And they grabbed in there all at once and got their hands in that mess! The coyote must have taken a physic. And these fellows were very angry. So they went after Coyote. They wanted to find that fellow.

But he was too far away, and they didn't have anything to eat. They were starving for a while there, and they all died.

### 28. *Coyote Steals Fire from the Birds*

In the beginning no one but the birds had fire. No others had it; no fire was allowed to any of them. And these birds had a fire in one big place only, on a big bluff, a round bluff I guess.

Coyote was coming from over this way, running around. He came to the place where the children of these birds were shooting arrows. And he began to play with those boys up on the side of the mountain where

---

[1] In another version more particulars are given concerning the bird. "It is red, yellow, and black, and it follows me all over and talks to me. It tells me anything I wish to know." These virtues are quite in keeping with Chiricahua ideas, for birds were often thought to act as monitors for human beings. In yet another version Coyote does not divulge what is under the hat but simply describes it as "pretty" and "good."

[2] A second version has Coyote demanding that he be allowed to cross four ridges before the hat is investigated.

the bluff was, shooting arrows. He won all the arrows from those little boys.

He asked these children, "Do you boys know the path that leads over this bluff?" And he said, "I know it. There's a place to go right over the bluff. I know where to go up." He didn't know it himself, but he wanted the boys to tell him about it. He just said this to get one of them to tell him so he could steal the fire.

The boys told him, "Our parents told us not to let anybody know where that path is."

"Well," he said, "I'll give half of these arrows to any boy who can tell me the way to get over this bluff."

But those children said, "No, our parents told us not to tell anybody."

He said then, "I'll give all the arrows to anyone who can tell me where you go up on the bluff."

Then the youngest boy there told him, "I know what to do and what to say to get over that bluff. You see that piñon tree just on the edge of that bluff. You tell that piñon tree to bend down over you, and then it goes up with you and you get up on the bluff."

Instead of giving that little boy all the arrows, Coyote gave him half of them and started for that tree. He wanted to be sure of it. And he went to that bluff over there and told the tree to bend down. It bent down four times, and then he was sure of it. Then he was certain he could go up on that piñon.

And he went down where those birds were on the big bluff there. He made an announcement to those people. He said, "Around this country they have killed all your enemies. They have told me to come down and tell you to have a big celebration tonight."[1]

And they listened closely to him and said, "All right."

So when night came they all gathered together. And they made four big rings around the fire of different classes of birds.

Then Coyote went away and pulled the bark off the juniper tree, the softest part, and he tied it under his tail so he could catch the fire with it.

Then they began to have this dance. Coyote got right in the middle, close to the fire, and he was dancing there by the fire all by himself. Every now and then he stuck his tail in the fire while they were having a good time. One of the birds told him, "Old man, you're going to burn your tail." And every time he put his tail in the fire, he looked back to see if it had caught fire.

They said to him again, "Old man, you're going to burn your tail."

And he answered, "Let it burn!" He said, "I feel so happy because all our enemies have been killed! I feel so happy, that's why I act this way."

---

[1] A successful war expedition was always followed by a victory dance.

But some of the birds suspected him. They said, "Friends, he is trying to get away with our fire."

And the coyote said, "I'm so happy! It's my way. I'm celebrating." Then he stuck his tail in the fire and held it there a long time and looked to see if the fire had caught on the brush he had there. Then he jumped over those four lines around him. His tail was on fire. And he ran with that fire. He dashed for that bluff where the piñon tree was, and he set fire to objects all over the country where he traveled. Some of those birds were hard at work trying to put out that fire. They were after him, and some were trying to put out the fire. But the wind began to blow, and the fire spread everywhere.

They couldn't put out the fire. Then they begged either Wasp or Hawk, I forget which one, to make it rain. And so it started to rain very hard. The rain was putting out all that fire.

But the coyote still had some fire burning. Coyote gave the fire to Bumblebee in a hole in a tree somewhere. And Bumblebee kept that fire in a hollow tree, kept it out of the rain. That's how they got fire, they say. And the Chiricahua used to say, "Under the coyote's tail it is scorched yellow." They say this is what caused it. And there is black on the end of the coyote's tail where it was burned.[1]

### 29. *Gopher Helps Coyote Have Intercourse with a Girl*

Well, you know, there was a bunch of pretty girls, prairie-dogs, playing the stave game. One of them was especially beautiful. Coyote came along and looked over the girls, and there was this one very pretty one.

This coyote went around to the gopher. He said, "You see that pretty girl sitting down there? Make a little hole right under her. I want to crawl right under that girl."

Gopher did just as Coyote said. Then Coyote crawled in there, right under that girl. He stuck his penis up directly under that girl. The girl felt something. She moved around.

"What's that? Something is under me!" She said.

Pretty soon she moved over and saw something sticking up. She

[1] A somewhat different version contains these deviations: The people have to eat raw meat because the prairie-dogs alone have fire. Coyote comes to the prairie-dogs' dance. He first drums for them, then gives up singing and dances. After obtaining fire he is chased by the prairie-dogs. He gives the fire to Fly. The prairie-dogs ask for aid and it begins to rain. Fly gives the fire to Bee who preserves it in his home in the yucca stalk. This is why yucca stalk is used for the fire drill; it has fire in it.

In still another version Coyote steals fire from the flies, passes it to Hummingbird, who hands it to Buzzard. Hoijer (*op. cit.*, p. 17) recorded a version in which Coyote steals fire from the flies and passes it on to Eagle. Wind blows and spreads the fire. The flies, who now hate Coyote, ask that the stones, earth, and water be made too hot for him. Because at that time any evil wish directed against anyone was gratified, this wish is granted and Coyote is tortured by the heat. He leaps into a pool of water, but it has become hot and he is scalded.

picked up that big center rock used in the game[1] and hit Coyote's penis with it. That is the reason the foreskin goes back, the Chiricahua say.

### 30. *Coyote as Eye Juggler*

The coyote was going along and he came to some rabbits playing.[2] This was under a very high bluff, this place where those rabbits were. And the rabbits were looking up there and throwing their eyes up. The eyes would go up and then come back into place.

Coyote said, "Oh, friends! What a pretty thing you are doing! Let me try it."

But the rabbits said, "No, you might lose your eyes."

Then Coyote said, "Please let me try." He just begged.

Pretty soon they got tired of him, and they threw his eyes up, and the eyes came back into the sockets again. They did this once and said, "That's enough for you."

And he said, "No, let me try it once more."

And they tried it again. They threw his eyes up again. Then the rabbits began to yell, "Let the eyes get stuck on something up there and not come back."

And his eyes did not come back.

### 31. *Coyote Dances with the Reeds*

So this coyote was blind, and he went to a swampy place. He came to some reeds at night. Reeds grow in bunches and when the wind blows they sway together. Coyote was walking along and he got in these reeds. The wind was blowing. He yelled and danced in the reeds. He danced with them all night. And in the morning he felt his way out and somehow came to a big camp of coyotes.

### 32. *Coyote Gets a Girl but Loses Her because of His Blindness*

Coyote came to a camp and he was telling those people stories of what a time he had been having with those Reed girls down at the black water. He said, "Those people surely had a good time last night! Those girls certainly had a lot of fun with me. Why, I never slept a wink last night! I'd better take a nap." He held his head down so they couldn't see that he was blind.

And when he woke up from his nap he asked for a drink of water. "Give me a drink of water." And they handed him water.

He said, "I have a habit of drinking nothing but fresh water from the spring." He wouldn't drink the water. Then he said, "Only a young girl in buckskin clothes who has never been married can get water for me."

[1] The center rock is the one against which the three staves are thrown in this game.

[2] In another version these are specifically identified as jack-rabbits.

Right away those people began dressing a girl in buckskin clothes. "Take that water jar down to the spring," they told her.

Coyote could hear the jingles on her clothes. And that girl went down to the spring, far off.

She had been gone only a little while when this blind coyote said, "I'm thirsty. I must drink now. How far is that spring?"

"Oh, straight ahead."

"I must go down right now."

When he got to the spring, this girl was still there. One way I've heard it is that he said, "I've just asked your people for you to be my wife. You must go my way." Another way I've heard it is that Coyote heard the jingles on the girl's clothes and grabbed her. He said, "Drop that jar! Your people just got killed! Take my hand and let's run!"

So they started to run. Coyote had a bow and arrows. He told that girl, "You know where the cattle go to water." He was guessing that she would know. She said she would show him. He was holding on to her all the time. There was only one way to go to the water, and they lay there where the cattle would come. He told her to hold the arrow even with the heart of a cow over there and then to tell him when to let it go. Now the cattle were coming to the water.

"There's one. Get ready," she said.

Coyote pulled the bow and she pointed the arrow.

"What have I done, my wife?"

"You missed it."

He missed every time. He shot at the last one and killed it. And after it was killed they began to butcher it.

All the time this girl was wearing the buckskin clothes with pendants on. He heard her all the time. If she ran he could catch her.

Coyote told his wife to build a fire close to the animal. He wanted to be near enough to his wife to hear if she should jump or run. He was butchering.

His wife saw that he was cutting a hole in the hide every time he cut. So she said, "Don't cut a hole in that hide. Be careful. It could be used for something. It's a nice hide." That's what the girl told him.

Then the coyote said, "When the knife is sharp you have to go every way with it." He cut out a piece of meat and said, "Here, put this in the fire. Cook it."

While the meat was cooking she was picking up sticks around the fire and was going to put the meat on those sticks. She told him to turn the meat over, and he went over there. He could hear that meat burning. He tried to pick up the meat, but he only picked up coals.

Then his wife looked closely into his face. Since his eyes were gone, the worms were beginning to drop from his eye sockets. He was blind. Then she folded up all her jingles and walked quietly away while he was picking up coals. When she was pretty far away she started to run from that man.

Coyote heard the jingles far away. And he started to run and shouted, "You think I don't see you? I see where you're going." And he took after her through the brush.

The girl pulled off one of her buckskin garments and put it over a little cluster of cactus. If he ran past it and touched it, it would jingle, she knew.

Just as he passed the buckskin dress it jingled and he jumped on it. He went right at it and began to have intercourse with the cactus.

He said, "This vagina must be made out of thorns!"

So that girl got away. And Coyote wandered somewhere from there, I don't know where.

### 33. *Coyote Shows How He Can Lie and Steals a Mule*

Well, this one coyote could tell more lies! All the other coyotes came to visit him. And all these other coyotes said to him, "Old man, tell us how you lie and how you make people believe your lies."

This coyote said, "It costs a great deal to learn how I lie and how I make others believe my lies. I like knowing how so much that I don't want to tell anybody. It's very valuable to me."

So the coyotes said, "We will give you anything you ask for if you will tell us."

"Well, it's going to cost you a good white horse with a new saddle on it and silver-mounted spurs. That's what it is going to cost you to find out how I lie and make people believe me."

Instead of a white horse they brought him a fine looking white mule which belonged to one fellow. It had a new saddle on. Coyote took it and began whipping it and trying to make it balk.

He said, "This mule doesn't act right. This mule is still balking for something."

Then they asked him, "What's he balking for?"

He said, "You must put something under this saddle. It's got to be a fine saddle blanket."

Then he got off and they put a saddle blanket on the mule. He got on it again. He was whipping it and holding back on it at the same time on purpose. It wouldn't move.

Coyote said, "This mule is still balking for something more."

They asked him what it was.

He said, "A silver-mounted bridle."

He got on the mule again and began whipping it a little and letting it take one or two steps at a time and then pulling back on it.

Again he said, "This mule is still balking for something."

They said, "What is it?"

He told them, "Silver-mounted spurs."

Then Coyote thought he had everything he could ask for, and he spurred the mule and rode out and left the crowd. He never went back over there and went off to a distant place where some other coyotes were playing hoop and pole. And he lost everything over there in the game and left that part of the country.[1]

### Variant Ending

Coyote knew that the man from whom he had got the mule had a gun and a horse. He wanted these. So he painted the mule black and took it back to the man next day. He said to the man (who now needed a mule), "I'll trade you this black mule for your horse and gun with ammunition."

The man traded. Coyote went off with the gun and horse. He had traded the man's own mule back to him for these.

Pretty soon it began to rain. The paint was washed off the mule and the man saw that it was his own mule.[2] Coyote took the gun and horse to the hoop and pole grounds and there lost them gambling at hoop and pole.[3]

### 34. Coyote Escapes Being Flayed by Inducing Another Coyote to Take His Place

This coyote had been doing a lot of mischief around a certain ranch, killing calves, or sheep, or goats, I guess, and these people went after him and ran him down and caught him. Then they took him home and they tied him up.

Then along came another coyote[4] and asked him, "What are you doing here with that rope on you, tied up?"

"Why these people love me so much that they feed me well here and give me everything I want. They promise that they're going to give me the very prettiest girl they have tomorrow. These people really like me very much. If you want to, you can take my place. You can get that girl if you want to. She's supposed to be a very pretty girl," he said.

Really the people were going skin Coyote, take his hide off and turn him loose. That was the plan of those people as I heard the story long

---

[1] Another version of this story can be summarized thus: Coyote agrees to work for a man but says he has to journey to his home to get his family first. The man offers the loan of his mule in order to expedite matters. Coyote so handles the mule that it seems afraid of him. In order to allay the fears of the mule Coyote has the man give him his hat, then his coat, then his boots, which Coyote successively dons. Then Coyote rides away, after laughingly denying a charge that he has supernatural power by means of which he frightens the mule. The man gives pursuit but succeeds only in falling and hurting himself. This incident is associated with the tale of Coyote and the "money tree" (story 26), for he sells the mule and uses part of the proceeds to deck out the "money tree."

[2] From another informant was obtained a variant of the episode of the painted horse. In it Coyote steals a white horse from his employer, paints it black, except for one white spot left on the forehead, and sells it. He is caught and put in jail.

[3] The hoop and pole game is an important gambling game of the Chiricahua in which a long pole is slid after a rolling hoop. The object is to make the hoop fall on the butt end of the pole.

[4] According to another version it is a dove which Coyote induces to take his place.

ago. They were going to do it next day. But this second coyote believed the story about the girl and was very eager to be tied there.

"Well then, untie me." He untied Coyote and was tied there instead. Some say that the people took this coyote's hide off. Others say that they put him in boiling water. I don't know which is true.

Well, the second coyote got away from there after they had him skinned, and he went to another coyote camp. And he was red all over, and he was sitting over there just as thin and cold as could be. Other coyotes looked at him. This was something new around their camps. He was over there by himself, and the other coyotes looked at him. And those coyotes yelled at him, "Hey, you with the red shirt!" He wouldn't look up. He was angry because they yelled about his red shirt. And they kept calling to him, "Hey, you with the red shirt!"

Then finally he looked at them, angry, half turning his head, and answered them. He said, "It's your father who has a red shirt!"[1] He was angry and walked off.

### 35. *Coyote and the Rats*

Some rats were pounding on the dry meat at their camp and along came a coyote.

He said, "Why is it you people are so busy pounding on dry meat? I heard someone calling out here; your sweethearts are calling out here. Do you know what they are saying to you?"

The rats told him, "You go away. Your talk is silly. We don't want you to talk to us and bother us."

So he went away.

### 36. *Coyote Kills Deer with His Ceremony*[2]

Next Coyote went to the deer family. There he talked to the deer, the head of the family. He said, "Old man, let's go out hunting some

---

[1] The informant explained that to make an insulting reference about a close relative of another was very serious, and would be considered more so if the person referred to happened to be dead.

[2] Another informant made two stories of this material. In the first of these two stories, Deer and Coyote go out hunting together. Coyote kills Deer, butchers him, puts some of the meat in a tree (a common Chiricahua usage), and carries the rest home. He passes Deer's home, inquires of Deer's wife whether Deer has come home, and voices fears for his safety because he has failed to come to an appointed spot. He gives a piece of meat to the woman; it is part of her own husband. That evening Coyote's wife goes to visit Deer's wife and unthinkingly blurts out, "That meat was your husband!" The second story of this pair is told about another deer who is wounded. Coyote offers to perform a rite for him, but plans to assure his death. He prepares poison to give the deer and tells his wife about it. That night Coyote and his wife go over to the camp of the sick deer. Coyote prays and sings. Then he tells his wife to go back for the medicine he has prepared. She asks him whether he means the poison. He curses her and denies that he wants such a thing. She catches the hint, however, and brings the poison. Coyote applies it and Deer dies.

deer." And the deer took up with him and said he would help him hunt deer.

But before they went out the coyote told the deer, "If someone happens to shoot you, don't look in either direction to see who did it." And he told him, "It will be just too bad for you if you do look!"

The coyote left his family with the deer family. He and Deer went out hunting. Coyote told Deer, "Old man, you go out this way, and I'll go the other way."

He had been watching the deer, his partner, all this time. This deer he was hunting with was a very fat deer.

They hadn't gone so very far when the coyote ambushed the deer down in a little canyon. He shot him right through the flank just as Deer was passing him. Then he hid and made a circle around back from where they had been coming. He acted as if he was trailing that deer. And he found that deer by his trail as if he was tracking him up to the place where he was. The deer was pretty badly hurt.

When Coyote got there he found that this deer was in very bad shape, and he told the deer, "Old man, I'll see what I can do for you. You be very still, and I'm going to sing for you."

So this coyote was singing for Deer. He began to sing and he sang, "Just about morning he will die."[1]

Deer got a hint of what Coyote was singing and said, "Old man, I'm pretty badly wounded and I heard you singing that I was going to die early in the morning."

And Coyote told him, "You didn't hear it right. When I sang, I said that just about morning you will get up and be well. You heard it wrong."

And Coyote helped him up and they started for home. He took him back to his family. And he told him, "I'm going to perform a ceremony for you tonight."

When night came this coyote began singing for Deer again. This deer and this coyote had camps close together. Now Coyote just happened to forget his medicine when he went to this deer's camp. So Coyote called to his wife.

His wife asked him, "What do you want?"

And he said, "Bring my medicine."

Before his wife thought of what he was trying to do, she said, "Which medicine do you want, the poison?" He had two kinds of medicine. One was poison; the other was one of the sunflowers. This is one of the best medicines the Apache have. It is used for wounds I think.

When his wife asked if he wanted poison, Coyote was angry and told her, "I wish a white man would come and hit you in the mouth with it!"[2]

---

[1] Ritual songs are important parts of Chiricahua curing ceremonies.
[2] This is a curse.

So then she yelled again, "Do you want the sunflower medicine?"
He said, "Yes," and added in a low tone, "the poison."

And then when she brought that poison he got after his wife right
before the deer family. He told his wife, "Why should you yell about
poisoned medicine? You ought to know better. This man is very, very
sick. You mustn't talk about poison when a man's very sick like this."[1]
That's what he said to his wife.

So he started his ceremony, singing for the deer. He told him, "Turn
over a little. I'll put some medicine on there." He had his medicine
in the form of a ground up powder. He picked it up and put it where the
wound was. Then he was performing a ceremony on the other side too.
And he sang. He sang the same song: "Just about morning he will
die." But he didn't say the words very distinctly.

The deer family was listening, and the mother asked, "What did
you say?"

"I said, 'Just about morning he will get well.' Don't meddle with
my singing. Don't say things that are bad."

And he kept singing that same song over and over. Then he went
away; he went home. In the morning the deer died.

After the deer was dead, Coyote told the deer family, "All right,
you go ahead and move your camp somewhere else. We'll fix him up
for you.[2] We'll take good care of him."

So this deer family went on. They were very sad. They went away.

And after they were gone far away the coyote and his family began to
eat up the deer. They went right at it. While the coyote and his family
were eating this deer, one of the coyote's little boys slipped a piece of
the entrails under his shirt.

The coyote family, after they had had enough to eat, followed this
deer family to the place where they had gone. They caught up with
them and they camped close to them. Coyote didn't have a fire, but
the deer family had a fire. So Coyote told one of his boys to go over and
borrow fire from that family.

He just happened to send the boy who had that piece of the entrails.
And while this little boy was out getting the fire, he leaned over and
dropped that piece of the entrails. The deer family saw it.

That little boy quickly excused himself. He said, "I dropped my piece
of entrails," and he picked it up quickly and went off with his fire.

### 37. *The Little Rabbits*

This is a very short story. It is about some little rabbits. They were
singing and playing. These little rabbits came out from the brush where
their hiding places were, and they played around there. They were
singing about themselves.

[1] To talk of evil or misfortune in these circumstances is to induce it, the belief runs.

[2] That is, "We'll attend to his burial."

"Little rabbit is out!
Little rabbit is out!"

That is what they were singing. And they were singing:

"I'll be the first coyote to swallow those rabbits."

The rabbits were singing that because Coyote hunts rabbits and swallows them in one gulp. They were singing about Rabbit and Coyote.

### 38. *Coyote Makes His Legs Thin Like Mink's Legs*

Coyote came to Mink. Coyote said to him, "What small legs you have! And you're so fast on them! How do you do it?" He wanted to try having his legs that way too.

Mink told him, "I took a knife and shaved off all the flesh on one side. That's what makes me go so lightly and so fast."

Coyote didn't wait to hear the rest. He ran for home. When he got home he sharpened his knife just as sharp as he could make it. Then he took the knife and shaved his leg muscles off to the bone on each side. He was bleeding. He tried to walk and he couldn't do it.

That's what makes the coyote's legs slim even now. Before this coyotes must have had fat muscles there.[1]

### 39. *Coyote and the Bird Girls*

Coyote was going along. He found some little birds. They were lying down in a nest. And he got directly above them and he dropped something heavy on them and killed every one of them. He went away after he had killed these birds, went away on a journey about his business.

He found some very pretty birds, four girls, lying down. They don't say what kind of birds they were. When Coyote saw these very pretty girls, four of them, lying down, he acted as if he stumbled, and he fell right on top of those pretty girls. He just did it on purpose.

And the girls cried, "Oh, my stomach!" He was rolling on them.

And Coyote said, "Every one of you keep still. I'll have intercourse with every one of you."

Then they got after him and he went away.

### 40. *Woodpecker Gives Coyote a Boy for Wife*

Then Coyote came to the home of Woodpecker. There were two woodpeckers. One of them was a young boy, but the other one dressed him up like a girl. Before this boy was dressed in girl's clothes, he picked up one of those turtle shells and put it between his legs.

[1] This story as related by a member of the Eastern Chiricahua band substitutes Jack-rabbit for Mink. The only significant change is that Jack-rabbit performs the "trimming" of the legs for Coyote. He has Coyote put his legs on a flat rock and tells him not to notice the pain, for soothing medicine is to be applied after the operation. He cuts the flesh to the bone, then breaks the bone with a rock and escapes.

Then Woodpecker said to Coyote, "I'm going to give you a very pretty girl. Do you want to marry her?" And there was that young fellow dressed up like a pretty girl.

Coyote said, "All right, I'll marry her."

It was a young boy, you know. And this boy was over there scraping a deer hide like a woman in order to deceive Coyote.[1] The other woodpecker was up there on a tree watching him.

While the boy was scraping off the hide, the coyote was having a hard time. Every now and then he reached under the dress and ran his hand up and grabbed the turtle shell. Oh, he just went wild! Pretty soon he was almost crazy. Then that bird flew up in the tree by the other one in the hole and left Coyote there.

The coyote stood under the tree. He kept saying, "Come down or I'll push the tree over!"

### 41. *Coyote Trades Tobacco for a "Girl"*

There was a big camp of coyotes. Only one coyote had tobacco. And so the others got together to plan how to get some of that tobacco. These men wanted very much to smoke, but they could get no tobacco from this man who had it.

This coyote was a single man. They could have given him a girl, but they played a joke on him. They took a boy and dressed him up in a buckskin dress. They painted him. A whole bunch of men took this boy, dressed as a girl, and brought him over to this man.

They told this man, "Old man, we came over here to speak to you. We all like you very much. We'll give you this girl if you'll give us your tobacco."

"Well," the coyote said, "all right." Then Coyote took out his tobacco and put it there by those men. He said, "Go ahead and smoke, and take home what is left."

He yawned even though it wasn't late. He said, "I'm sleepy, very sleepy. I've been out all day and I'm tired." It wasn't late, but he said that.

And that boy with the buckskin dress was lying down on his bed. Every now and then Coyote would lie beside his "girl." He was restless and eager. He said, "I'm sleepy." He kept saying that over and over.

The other coyotes tried to shame him. They said to one another, "The old man is pretty sleepy. Let's leave him alone." They took the tobacco and went.

They all went out, nudging each other and laughing on the way.

Before some of those men had even reached their camps, Coyote put up those buckskins and began to try to have intercourse right away. He was feeling around between that boy's legs.

"Don't get hold of my penis," the boy told him.

[1] Note the reference here to division of labor based on sex.

The coyote ran out and the boy jumped out and went home laughing.

Coyote ran outside and cried, "You men who gave me this 'girl,' you'd better come and get your 'girl' and bring back my tobacco!"

He was angry about it. He was ashamed of himself. That night he left that part of the country.

### 42. *Coyote Kills His Rival by Making Him Swallow Hot Stones*

One coyote had a very pretty wife. And this coyote was out hunting. His pretty wife was unfaithful to him all the time. One day while he was out hunting he killed a deer very early. He came back and was carrying it close to his camp rather quietly. Another coyote was so busy with the man's wife that he didn't hear the husband coming up to the camp.

While they were having intercourse in there the wife was saying (and Coyote was listening outside), "Oh, it's good, good!" And the other coyote on top of her was saying, "Is it good?" And she was saying, "Yes, good, good!"

So her husband untied all that meat and pushed it off and said, "This is good, too!" And he ran in there and caught them.

He said, "All right, you sit over there." He was talking to both of them. He told his wife, "You get out there and get four stones and put them on the fire right here. Let them get hot, red hot!"

And she went out quickly and brought in four stones. She put them in the fire and got them red hot.

Then her husband told that coyote, "Now, old man, you swallow those four rocks. If those rocks don't kill you, I'll walk out of here and you can have anything that's in here, my wife and all."[1]

So that coyote licked his lips and rubbed his hands. "I'm a shaman," he said, "I'm a good shaman."[2]

Coyote said, "All right, that stone is hot. You eat it."

Then the other spat on his hands and said, "I'm a shaman."

And the husband got a stick and pushed a hot stone out to him and told him, "Get hold of it quickly and swallow it." He was ordering that fellow around. If he didn't do as he was told, the husband was going to kill him right there.

So the other picked up that stone. He said, "I used to be a shaman." He swallowed the stone. It went down. Then the husband pushed another stone out. He didn't give him much time. The fellow took it. He made the same statement and did as he had the first time. He did the same thing three times. The fourth time he said, "I used to be a sha—." He just about said that and he fell dead.

---

[1] For this same motif, associated with the story of the man who was sent up on a rock, see footnote 2, p. 28.

[2] Legerdemain, including exhibitions with fire, were not unknown among the Chiricahua shamans.

The coyote said, "Drag that fellow out. He stinks. Drag him into the brush."

And his wife dragged that other one out and threw him out there somewhere. When she got back she looked as though she had been crying.

And her husband said, "It looks as though you have been crying."

She said, "No, a little branch whipped my eyes. That's what makes the tears run down."[1]

He said, "You clean up the place where he's been sitting."

### 43. *Goldfinch Causes Coyote to Fall out of a Tree*

This coyote was going along, and he looked up in the top of a tree. There was a bird's nest up there, a goldfinch's nest. He climbed up there where the nest was, and the bird was in there.

And he said to the bird, "What a pretty place you have up here! What a fine nest!" And he asked him, "Where's your toilet?"

Goldfinch told him, "See that little branch over there? You can sit over there if you want to."

Coyote started to sit on those branches at the end of the limb, and he fell off.[2]

### 44. *Coyote and Dog Argue*

Some dogs were out in the woods. Some coyotes came to the dogs.

One coyote said, "Why don't you dogs come and join us out in this wilderness? We live out here, happy, free. We eat all kinds of wild fruits. No one abuses us. We live among the little bushes and live very happily, free from getting whipped or scolded."

The dog said, "No, we live with some people and they take good care of us. We live on meat and fat which they bring us. We sleep in a camp with these Indians. They tell us, 'My dog, I love you.' They take very good care of us."

Then the coyote told him, "We've heard you dogs from these hills; they have been whipping you dogs, and we have heard you crying over there."

Then the dog said to the coyote, "We all have to learn to obey our masters. Sometimes we don't obey; that's the only time we get a whipping."

Coyote said, "They whip you just the same."

Dog told them, "You live out in the woods and have many enemies."

Coyote said, "We eat nothing but fat out in the woods, all kinds of meats are what we eat. We eat prickly pears, yucca fruit, and all kinds of wild fruits." Then Coyote told him, "We hear you get whippings all the time anyhow. We hear you crying all the time they are whipping you."

[1] For a similar motif associated with another story see p. 31.
[2] For the use of a similar theme in another story see p. 67.

But the dog said, "We get plenty of meat and a good place to sleep. We do not have to dodge anyone the way you do. We cannot agree with you that we should go back to the woods with you."

### 45. *Coyote Eats Mouse and Breaks Wind*

Coyote went to a little mouse. He said, "You are pretty fat. You'll make good eating. I've eaten all I have. I'm hungry and I'm going to eat you right now."

The little mouse didn't know what to say. Finally he told Coyote, "If anyone eats me he will have to break wind and will be sick."

"Oh, that doesn't bother me. I break wind anyway."

"This is an altogether different kind of breaking wind. It will make a loud noise and you will be ashamed before a big crowd." This part of the story explains why people are ashamed to break wind in a big crowd now and try to hold it.

"I'm not going near a crowd; I don't care," said Coyote.

"Well, you'll bounce around if you eat me. You'll have to hold on to something."

"Oh, I don't care. I break wind all the time."

Coyote ate the mouse. Then he began to get sick. He had to break wind. He ran to a bush and hung on. It bounced him around. He ran to another. He had to keep going in this way. He grew very sick. He had to vomit. He tried it in vain. He defecated a little bit and took the excrement on two fingers and put them far down his throat. Then he vomited out the mouse and was relieved.[1]

### 46. *Coyote Obtains Wood for Arrows and a Bow*[2]

Coyote was looking for wood for arrows. He found some Apache plume, but when he got there he found many rattlesnakes around it. He set fire to the grass around there and some of the snakes were burned. The rest had to go away. Then he cut arrow shafts for himself.

[1] Some say that he thrust his finger up his rectum and then down his throat to force the vomiting. Some say he put his fingers down his throat alone to do it. (Inf.)

[2] This story is supposed to account for the origin of the bow and arrow. Variants relate that Bear was guarding the mulberry tree. (Mulberry is the favorite bow wood among the Chiricahua.) In order to induce Bear to leave his post, Coyote tells him that fruit is ripe on a nearby mountain. When Bear demands proof, Coyote defecates, and fruit is to be seen in his feces. Before Bear returns Coyote has scattered the mulberry wood to the four directions and has made himself a bow.

One informant followed this story of the obtaining of bow and arrows with that entitled "Coyote Kills Deer with his Ceremony" (p. 58), the thread of continuity being that Coyote, now in possession of these weapons, goes out to hunt with them. In this version, however, Deer's wife, after Coyote has shot and killed her husband, builds a pit where Coyote usually sits when he comes visiting and covers it with brush and dirt. Coyote falls into the trap and is covered with dirt. Thus Deer is avenged.

Then Coyote was looking for a certain wood out of which to make a bow. It was the mulberry tree he was looking for. When he found it, there were many snakes around it too. He did the same thing. He set fire to the grass and the snakes had to get away. So he got bow wood too.

### 47. *Coyote Lets Darkness Out of the Sack*

Some man had a little sack in which darkness was tied up.[1] He gave it to Coyote and told him, "Don't open this sack, for if you do it is going to be dark."

Coyote kept it for a while without opening it. Then he opened the sack just a little, but the darkness got out and he could hardly see. Then it was dark all over.

### 48. *Coyote Rides Across the River in Cow's Rectum*

Coyote wanted to go across a river when the water was high. He couldn't swim and there was no way to get across. He sat down and waited.

Some cattle came to the water and one of them asked Coyote, "Why do you sit there?"

Coyote told her what was the trouble.

"Do you want me to help you?"

"Yes."

"Then sit on my head and hold on to my horns."

"No, I am afraid of being washed off."

"Then hold on to my tail."

"No, I'm afraid of being washed off from there too."

"I don't know how to help you then."

"Well, let me get in your rectum."

"All right," said the cow, "I'll let you get in there."

Coyote got in. The cow swam across with him and just as the cow made the other shore and was about to climb to the bank, Coyote bit her in there and killed her. Then Coyote came out and helped himself to the meat.

### 49. *Two Coyotes Vie for a Slain Cow*

One time Coyote killed a cow. About that time another coyote came up and begged for a piece. They agreed to bet. The one who could jump over the cow without touching it was to have it.

The second coyote jumped and didn't touch. Then the one who had killed the cow jumped over and touched. So the second coyote got it and told the other to get away. He took the meat, cut it in pieces, and put it in a big pine tree. The coyote who had lost the bet went home,

---

[1] In another version Badger is said to have the sack. (Cf. also this motif in the account of the moccasin game, footnote 1, p. 27.) Despite Badger's warning, Coyote, when Badger is not looking, unties a number of small bundles contained in the bag. After a time it becomes dark all over.

got his three children, and came back. They all begged for something to eat.

The coyote who was up in the tree told them all to lie on their backs and close their eyes. "I am going to throw you a big piece of meat," he said.

All did as they were told but the smallest coyote. He peeked. Instead of throwing meat down, the coyote in the tree hurled a big bone at them. Only the youngest one who was peeking was able to jump away and save himself. The others got killed.

This little coyote stayed under the tree and begged to be allowed to come up. Finally the big coyote told him to come. The little one sat up there and every time the big coyote turned his head away, he would grab a piece of meat. He grabbed a little at a time when the other was not looking, and he kept it up until he got very full. Then he had to relieve himself.

"Where's your toilet?" he asked.

The big coyote pointed to a long branch. "Go right out there at the end."[1]

The little one went out about half way. "Right here?" he asked.

"No, further."

He went out a little more.

"No, further."

He got to the very end and was just ready to relieve himself when the other shook the tree. The little one fell down and burst his stomach.

Big Coyote went down and found all that meat there. "I wonder where he got all that meat," he said.

### 50. *Coyote Tries to Catch Turkey by Diving for His Reflection in the Water and by Chopping Down Trees*[2]

Coyote was going along a river. There was a lot of water flowing and by the bank stood a tall tree. In this tree a turkey was sitting and his reflection showed in the water. Coyote saw this reflection and thought the turkey was in the water.

Without waiting, he jumped into the water. He could not find the turkey and came up. When he got to the bank he saw that the turkey was still there. He dove into the water again and kept it up for as long as he could stand it. Finally he was so tired that he had to stop and lie

---

[1] For this same motif as a separate story see p. 64, "Goldfinch Causes Coyote to Fall out of a Tree."

[2] Another version prefaces this story by the tale found on p. 69 of this cycle, "Turkey Escapes from Coyote." In this variant another familiar theme is added at the end. After tiring himself by chopping down trees Coyote lies on his back and rests in the shade. He sees clouds moving through the trees and it appears to him that the tree is falling on him. He runs to an arroyo. This is the utilization of a motif much like that which appears in "Coyote Helps Lizard Hold up the Sky," p. 37.

on his back to rest. He rolled over on his back, and as he did so he saw the turkey up in the tree.

Coyote was very angry when he saw this. He ran and got an axe and began to chop down that tree. But when that tree fell, Turkey flew to another tree. Coyote went to this tree and chopped it down too, but Turkey just went on to another one. Coyote kept this up till he was so worn out that he had to give up, and Turkey got away.[1]

### 51. *Coyote Lives with the Ant People and the Mouse People*

There was a deep canyon with water in it and high cliffs all around. The ant people and the mouse people lived there. When Coyote came to that place and stood above the canyon, he met a row of the ant people strung out and following one another down. Some of them asked him to go down with them.

"But I won't be able to get up again," Coyote said.

"Oh, we'll help you get up," they told him.

So he agreed to go and the ants helped him down. When he got down there, a big dance was going on and he had a good time.

He stayed with these people a long time. But finally he wanted to go up to his home, to his own poeple. But he couldn't find the way out. He made up his mind he was going to get out. He thought that if these people knew what his purpose was, they would not let him go. He saw the ants start to go up the side of the cliff. He followed them, unseen, but the place they went up was too steep for him.

So he went back to the mice. "I've been here a long time," he said. "I ought to go up and see my people for a short visit soon. But I don't want to be away for long, I like it so well here. The next time you mice go up, I believe I'll go with you."

"Have you ever tried to go up?" they asked him.

He told them, "No." though he had tried many times. He was making believe he was not glad to go. "I'll go with you if you stay for just a little while. I'll go with you if you come back before dark, for I can't get down in the dark."

When the mice went up the next time he went with them. They helped him, pushed him up. As soon as he got on top he saw smoke in the distance. He told the mice he was going over there. "I'll be back. Be sure to wait here for me," he told them. "I'd like you to come with me but you can't run as fast as I can."

He went to the camp he had seen from the distance. They were having a dance there and he joined them. He told them he had come from the country of the mice and ants and that he would sing mouse songs for them that night. He did and he stayed with these people a long

---

[1] This motif is used also as a separate story (see "Coyote Tries to Catch Turkey by Chopping down Trees," p. 41). The motif of diving for a reflection in the water has been encountered before in episode 12 of the Coyote cycle, p. 39.

time. He said, "The ants talked the Navaho language, so they must be Navaho."[1]

### 52. *Coyote Tries to Count the Prairie-Dogs*

Once Coyote killed a great many prairie-dogs. He hid them under the grass and went off to find his children and bring them to eat the food. When he got back with the children he looked at the pile of prairie-dogs. It looked to him as though some were missing. So he started to count them and he counted in a funny way, *"le'i, čutas, čutas, čudis, 'aččus."*[2] He kept saying these first five numbers over and over; then he couldn't count any more. He repeated these words over and over but he couldn't get above five. Then he said to his children, "Well, anyway, eat them!"

### 53. *Turkey Escapes from Coyote*[3]

Coyote went hunting and caught a wild turkey. "Go to my camp," he told this turkey, "and tell my wife to kill you and have you ready for supper about dark." Then Coyote went on.

Turkey went over to Coyote's house and told Coyote's wife that he was sent by her husband with the order that all the sinew should be taken, the bowstrings and other things, and cooked up for supper.

When Coyote came home he expected a good supper. His wife put the cooked sinew before him.

"What's the matter?" said Coyote in anger. "Didn't that fellow come over and tell you what to do?"

"Yes, he came over and told me to do just what I have done. He told me to cook up all the sinew around here for your supper."

Coyote got very angry. *"bešdacada!"* he said.[4] He used very bad language.

### 54. *Coyote's Bearskin Quiver Comes to Life and Chases Him*

The coyote, who killed all the others, went into the woods. There he found some bears and he shot and killed one. He took the hide, and, after drying it, he wanted to make a quiver of it.

Someone came to see him. "What are you going to do with that?" he asked.

"Make a quiver of it."

"You'd better not do it. You are not supposed to do that."[5]

---

[1] That the Navaho are somehow associated with the ants is a notion that the writer has a number of times encountered among Apache groups. (See (e), p. 101, for a further development of the idea.)

[2] The names for the numerals which Coyote uses are not the ordinary terms but are nonsense words from the repetition of which the informant derived a great deal of merriment.

[3] For another reference to this motif see footnote 2, p. 67.

[4] Literally, simply "knife and awl," but it has the force of a curse.

[5] The Chiricahua are very much afraid of the bear and a serious sickness is thought to come from this animal. Bear hide was not to be touched and bear flesh was not eaten.

"I'm going to do it."

"Then harm will surely come to you."

But Coyote made a quiver and a carrier for his bow of the hide, and when it was finished he put it on his back. He walked along until he came to a walnut tree. There were many nuts on the ground and some on the tree. He took his quiver off and put it against the tree and began to pile up the walnuts.

The quiver began to come to life and was shaking. He heard the rustling, but he said to himself, "Oh, it's just the wind," and paid no attention.

But finally the skin turned to a live bear again, and the bear chased him. He ran through thick brush until he was tired out. And he was just about to give up when he saw a gopher.

"What are you running for?" Gopher asked.

"Bear is about to catch me. Help me!"

"Go into my mouth," Gopher said.

Coyote ran into Gopher's cheek pouch and it looked as if Gopher's mouth were all swelled up. Just then Bear came up.

He asked, "Did you see anyone run this way?"

"No."

"What have you got in your mouth?"

"Teeth."

Bear kicked Gopher and Coyote fell out. Bear ran after Coyote again, but he got away.

### 55. *Coyote Makes Woman Valuable by Breaking the Teeth in Her Vagina*

One time Coyote found a very pretty woman. He tried to make love to her. He took her in the woods on a walk. He wanted to have intercourse with her and was just about to do so when he saw teeth in her vagina. He was afraid. When she wasn't looking he got a stick and a long slender rock.

First, instead of putting his penis in, he put in the stick, and it was ground up. Then he put the rock in, and the teeth were knocked off until her vagina became just as a woman's is now. After that he had intercourse with her.

Then the woman said, "Hereafter I shall be worth a lot. I am worth horses and many things now."

That is why men give horses and different things when they marry women today.

### 56. *Coyote Tries to Spot His Children like Fawns*

Coyote found two little new-born deer. They were spotted and he liked very much the way they looked. He came to their mother. "Tell me," he asked her, "how did you get your children so nice and spotted?" And he told her, "I should like to fix my children the same way."

The mother told him, "It's not very hard to do. Find a little cave in the rocks and put your children in it. Then heap juniper wood out in front of it. Set fire to the wood. That wood sputters and pops and spots the children."

Coyote went home. He called his children. He stood them in a cave and filled the entrance up with juniper. He set fire to it and went away. When he came back he found that he had killed all his children.

### 57. *Coyote Eats Berries and Goes Up in the Air*[1]

Coyote was going along the road another time. He came to a tree with many berries on it. Bear was sitting beside it. Coyote wanted to eat some of the berries, but Bear wouldn't let him.

Bear said, "No, you can't eat those berries. I am here to guard this tree. If you eat these berries it will make you jump higher and higher into the air until you get sick. That's why I'm watching."[2]

Coyote did not believe what the bear told him. He wanted to eat those berries. But he said nothing; he just sat down under the tree and waited.

After a while Bear said to him, "Watch this tree for me. I'm going for water and will be right back. Don't let anyone eat any of this fruit."

So Bear went to get a drink and as soon as he was out of sight, Coyote began to eat some of the berries. He stopped before Bear came back, and when Bear reached the tree, Coyote was again sitting down.

But suddenly Coyote jumped up into the air. Then he did it for a second time, only higher. Then a third time, even higher. He begged the bear to hold him down but the bear wouldn't help him. Finally he recovered.

Coyote left that place at once. He went along the trail again till he came to another tree like that, covered with ripe fruit. He wanted some but he was afraid to try it. He sat for a long time under that tree trying to make up his mind. Then he went on.

### 58. *Coyote Story Fragments*

A number of Coyote story fragments or summaries of themes were obtained from Chiricahua informants by the writer and others. These are outlined here for the sake of completeness.

(a) Coyote puts on wings like Goose's and tries to fly with the geese. A variant of this has to do with some turkeys who lend Coyote wings. After he has made several successful flights they pull his wings from him and he falls, shouting.

(b) Coyote is lying in the reeds and is told to remain there, for a dance is to be held nearby. He naps and when he wakes up the bushes

---

[1] See footnote 2, p. 65 where Bear is also guarding a tree, a mulberry tree. In a variant of this story it is specifically stated that this tree of the dangerous fruit is a mulberry tree too.

[2] Cf. p. 65 where Coyote is told he will "bounce around" if he eats Mouse.

are on fire. He crawls through the flames but his back is scorched. This accounts for the black mark he shows there today.

(c) Coyote puts his moccasins on the wrong feet. When his attention is called to this he claims, in order to avoid ridicule, that he meant to put them on that way.

(d) Coyote puts something over his face to disguise himself and has sexual intercourse with a woman. Her pubic hair pricks him and he asks her whether she has burrs there. Then he jumps away and reveals himself, much to the consternation of the woman.

(e) Coyote sees cowboys roping horses. They have one end of the lasso around their waists. He asks for a rope, ties one end around his waist, and ropes a horse. The horse starts to run and drags Coyote, who bumps along with tail in air. The cowboys follow and find Coyote's bones and entrails along the trail. One tells another what he has found but opines that Coyote must still be holding on to the horse with other parts of his body. This motif usually appears as a Foolish People story for other Apache groups.

(f) Coyote sees cowboys roping wild cattle. He induces them to catch one for him that he may ride it. He mounts the animal and is soon thrown. The animal returns to Coyote and gores him.

## C. Animal, Bird, and Insect Tales

### 1. *The Geese Who Went on a Journey*[1]

Old Nani[2] used to tell a story about the geese. He said that some old men used to tell him when he was young about how some geese started from the north. Each of them had twelve pieces of bread. They were going far to the south. A large group went. They kept going for twelve days without stopping and then they got there.[3]

### 2. *Rat and Mouse Argue*

Rat and Mouse had a quarrel. Rat piles a lot of sticks up to live in. Mouse said to him, "You have a bad home. All you have are some things piled up there."

Rat answered, "My food doesn't make people sick. People can come

---

[1] A journey of the geese, in which Coyote participates, is often related by Apache tribes as an episode in the Coyote cycle. That the Chiricahua had such a story, though it has not been recorded in full, is indicated in (a), p. 71.

[2] Nani was leader or chief of the Eastern Apache band (Warm Springs).

[3] Power from Goose comes from heaven and not from earth, Nani used to tell us. Nani knew goose ceremonial songs. When men who know it get a goose feather they keep it for ceremonial use. (Inf.) Supernatural power from the goose is associated in Chiricahua ideology with speed and endurance in traveling. That is probably why the best known story of these birds has to do with a journey they took.

around even though I pile up snake bones.[1] You live in a dirty hole. Anybody who eats your food gets sick."

### 3. *The Robber-Fly People*

Robber-flies were people once. And they talked just as we do. Robber-fly has something that looks like a lump on his back.

He said, "You think this is a hump on my back, but it's the way I carry my meat." He sang a song then. He sang:

"I'm carrying liver on my back.
The people think I've got a hump,
But it is meat."

---

[1] The Chiricahua believe that a serious sickness, marked by emaciation and sores, is contracted from the snake. Why snake bones piled up by Rat should not injure people is not clear.

## IV. STORIES OF SUPERNATURAL BEINGS AND ENCOUNTERS WITH SUPERNATURALS

### A. THE GAHE

#### 1. The Disabled Boys Cured by the Gahe.

The Gahe have great power and the old people used to tell many stories about them. They have power like Child-of-the-Water. What I shall tell happened a long time ago when the Apache didn't know anything about Whites or Mexicans. There were many Chiricahua then. There were the Central Chiricahua, the Southern Chiricahua, and the Eastern Chiricahua.

At that time there was a boy born with no eyes in his face. And another was born with eyes but with no legs.[1] The people carried them around till they were about eighteen years old. Then they got tired of it. They had no horses and they had to move a long distance. The women carried big bundles then and had to put the children on top of the bundles. These two boys were in the way. So the people left them and moved a long distance away. They left the boys with a water jar filled with water but with no food.

The boys talked of what to do. The one with legs said, "I'll carry you and you watch where we are going. Tell me how to keep the trail and we'll follow the people."

So they started. They ran out of water and were almost dying of thirst. They were just ready to die when the Gahe came to them.[2]

The Gahe took them to the mountain in which they lived. Many people came together there. Many people lived in that mountain. They dressed all kinds of Mountain Spirits for these boys. They prayed and they began to sing. There were women in the mountain too. The women made the sound, the cry of applause, as they do at the big tipi during the girl's puberty rite now.

The boys prayed to the Gahe. The blind one asked to see. The one with no legs asked to have legs. Then clouds came, and lightning and thunder. The boys were covered with black clouds. You couldn't see the boys. Then the black clouds disappeared and the boys were there. The one who had lacked eyes had eyes now and the other boy had legs. Many Gahe were dancing.

After the boys got their eyes and legs, the Gahe asked them, "Would you like to go back to your own people now?"

[1] For a story in which the Gahe cure an old blind woman who has been abandoned and grant her the right to perform their ceremony see Hoijer, *op. cit.*, p. 33.

[2] In the short version obtained by Hoijer (*op. cit.*, p. 35) it is stated that Gray One (Clown) was the first of the Gahe to meet them and that it was he who led them back to the home of these Mountain Spirits.

The boys said, "Yes."

The Gahe told them where their people were living now. The Gahe told them to go to the top of a mountain near the camps of the people. "Then call to them and tell them who you are, but don't let them come to you for four days."

The boys did what they were told. They went to the mountain and called. The people called back and asked, "Who are you?" When they told them, the people came running but the boys made them stop and wouldn't let them come near for four days.

At first the people couldn't believe that these were the boys they had left behind. But the boys told them what had happened and just where they had been left behind. Then the boys called their fathers and mothers.

This story shows that there are people in the mountains who are just like us. They are not Gahe, but they make Gahe just as we do here. Those they make can take off their Gahe clothes and dress as we do. We hear the people drum in there and hear the Gahe dancing too. We hear words in there when we listen at cliffs or mountains, but we can't see the people. We call all these people in there Mountain People. They live in these mountains and have many children. There are girls, boys, women, and old men there. They are just like us. The real Gahe are the Gahe of these people.[1] The Mescalero talk about them too. There is a place right across in the Sacramentos, a big deep place. If you go there about sunset you can hear the drumming sometimes.

## 2. *The First Masked Dancer Ceremony*

After the flood there were many, many Indians. These Indians were very religious. They were careful how they used their language. They wouldn't ever dare to say, "I wish that dog would bite you," or "I wish that coyote would get you." They wouldn't ever dare say things like that.[2] They were afraid to tell lies.

Before this the Gahe were never known. There were many Chiricahua in a big camp. There was only one man among many thousand Indians who knew the Gahe. For some time the rest of the Chiricahua were not aware that he did know the ceremony. But they found out then that there was this one man who knew how to make masked dancers. It was something new to them. After the whole tribe found out, he came out with it. They called this man over and asked him what good it was.

---

[1] This explanation will serve to place the Gahe in Chiricahua religion. The Chiricahua believe that a race of supernaturals inhabits the interiors of certain mountains. These supernaturals occasionally dress and paint and cover the faces of some of their members. Such masked and decorated supernaturals become the pattern after which a Chiricahua "makes" his masked dancers after he has had a supernatural experience with these Mountain People. The Gahe or masked dancers of the Chiricahua function mostly to cure disease and are considered particularly efficacious in driving away epidemics. They also appear, principally for the entertainment of the spectators, at the girl's puberty rite.

[2] For fear they would therefore occur.

"All right," he said, "I'll tell you. I know the Gahe. I'm going to make that masked dancer ceremony for you tomorrow, and we're going to dance here for four nights."

He said, "See that mountain over there. I'm going to make these masked dancers off in the brush by that mountain, not near your camps. And all you people help out, right here on this flat. Bring wood while I'm fixing those dancers over there.

"And since I'm going to do this, I'll tell you the rules. I need three or four men to paint these dancers. And these men and the masked dancers I'm going to paint are the only ones I will allow over there. I'm telling you this for your own good, every one of you, men, women, and children. All of you stay away from the place where I'm going to make masked dancers. Keep your children away on the other side of the camp. I'm going to put paint on men who are living on earth, but if you know them, don't call their names. It is dangerous."[1]

Everyone knew that what this man said was for their own good and for the good of the children.

The man told them, "I have warned you. If any dangers come to you after what I have told you, it won't be my fault." Then he went over there to paint those dancers.

As I said, there were many Indians, and I suppose many children. At one camp there was a girl, eleven or twelve years old, who drifted off from the place where the children were playing.[2] She went over there. She crept up to those people who were being painted. She watched. She knew one of the men by name. She went back.

Evening came. All the people gathered around the fire to see the dance. It was the first time they had ever seen masked dancers going through the ceremony that they still do today.

Then the masked dancers began to dance. The man who knew the Gahe was singing. He started to sing, sang a little, and stopped. No one, not even the parents of the child, knew that that girl had been over there. She never told that she had been over there. But this man stopped for a moment. He said, "Listen to me closely. I have warned you, but what I warned you against has happened." He said, "One of the little girls of a certain family went over there and saw one of those men, and she knows who one of those men is. She called that man by name a moment ago when the dancers were going around the fire. She is in danger of being killed and taken away from us right here where everybody can see. But I'm going to do my best to prevent it. If I fail, I can't help it."

He sang songs to the Gahe to prevent it as the dance went on. The one who talked to him said, "Your only chance is to dig a hole right

---

[1] This prohibition against calling the name of the masked dancer is still observed.

[2] In two other versions which are at hand it is a little boy who spies on the masked dancers.

under the dance fire and put the girl in there." The man announced that he had been told what to do.

He told them, "The Gahe are coming from the mountain, not any men dressed up. And they will look for the child."

A short time afterward the Gahe came. They were not men from the tribe. They came from the mountains. They told the other dancers, the dressed up men, to go away. They wanted to take the ground. The first night they worked for a little while.

The first one was Great Blue Gahe, the second was Great Yellow Gahe, the third was Great Black Gahe. There were many of them, and the last was the clown.[1] They all carried, not sticks, but steel sabres.[2] But they had designs on just like the masked dancers that you see now.

They came around the fire once. They worshipped the fire.[3] And the girl was in there. They were trying to find the girl. From the east they went around four times next and then once more. Then they did the same thing from the south and from the other directions. Every time they got to the fire the leader dug up the fire as though he almost knew what was in there. But they couldn't find that girl there. These Gahe went all over camp, turning over bedding and brush and looking for that girl. Toward morning these Gahe went back to the mountain. And in the meantime the shaman was using all his power to prevent them from finding that girl.

On the first night it was Great Blue Gahe who was in the lead. He failed. The second night Great Yellow Gahe took the lead, and Great Blue Gahe came second last. The clown stayed last. They went through the same ceremony but could not find the girl. The third night Great Black Gahe came first and Great Yellow Gahe third. Clown was last. But Great Black Gahe couldn't find the girl either.

The fourth night the clown was in the lead. The three days before the clown took the lead, they went all around the hills, in the brush, and everywhere, but they failed to find the girl. The clown took the lead this night. The fourth time around from the east, the clown put his stick in the fire. The fourth time from the north he went right into that fire

[1] When the masked dancers approach the fire around which they dance, they come in single file. The narrator is describing the order in which they moved when in single file. Even though the members of a group of masked dancers are identically dressed and designed, each is associated with a different color and direction. The ideal arrangement is to have a set of four Gahe as follows: Great Black Gahe of the east, Great Blue Gahe of the south, Great Yellow Gahe of the west, and Great White Gahe of the north. In this story Gray One or Clown takes the place of Great White Gahe and the order in which the Gahe participate in the ceremony is somewhat unusual.

[2] In a variant it is said that these Gahe carried sticks which turned to sabres when the child was discovered.

[3] To worship the fire the Gahe approach it from the cardinal directions, beginning with the east and moving clockwise. From each direction they come to the fire in single file four times, swaying and uttering a peculiar call as they advance.

and pulled the girl out by the hair.[1] All the people saw them. The Gahe came around with their sabres and cut her to pieces for what she had said.[2]

### 3. *The Gahe Who Fought the Mexican Soldiers*[3]

This happened right at the foot of the Chuchillo Mountains, near the place where the woman was killed by the bear. A party of Warm Springs Apache were here, going back to the mountain. They were on the plains near the mountain. Mexican cavalry came after them. The Indians had no guns; they had nothing but bows and arrows and spears. They couldn't hurt anyone from a distance with these, but the soldiers had guns and could kill from a distance.

One man and a few women got away though the soldiers surrounded the Apache. The man prayed to the Gahe of the mountain as he ran. Then Gahe came out from the mountain, many of them. They surrounded the soldiers. They opened a cave in the rocks and with their swords drove the soldiers into the cave. Then they shut the door again and not one of the soldiers ever got out. They say there are shoes piled up at the mouth of the cave yet to show where the soldiers were driven in.

All the Gahe have real swords like the ones soldiers have. They had them at this time, and every time the Indians see the Gahe, they have real swords, they say.

### 4. *The Visit of the Gahe*

A great many Apache were camped together. Of all of them only one knew the ceremony of the Gahe. This man spoke to the people and said, "I will make Gahe for you. The ceremony will last four nights." Everyone was happy about it.

When the sun began to go down the Gahe were being decorated. By sunset they had built a big fire where the Gahe were to dance. All the men and women were gathered there.

The Gahe came to the fire. They worshipped it and went around it. The singing had begun and the Gahe danced. It was a great celebration.

[1] A good many Chiricahua believe that the clown, when he has serious tasks to perform, is the most powerful of the Gahe. For a summary of the position and function of the clown in Chiricahua ritual see Opler, "The Sacred Clowns of the Chiricahua and Mescalero Apache Indians," *El Palacio*, March, 1938, pp. 75–79.

[2] One informant claimed that the manner in which the masked dancers of the Chiricahua approach the fire, "running in toward the center as if they are grabbing someone," represents a dramatization of the fate of the child who did not pay them fitting respect. Another informant averred that it is dangerous even to tell stories of the Gahe and that to decrease the hazard, ceremonial names, such as "mountain people" are introduced into the tales in which they appear.

[3] This is a very popular story with the Chiricahua and is often told to emphasize the protective function of the Gahe. In one version it is said that the Mexicans also prayed to the Gahe and offered all their possessions, but to no avail. Another detail, appearing in a variant, is that the Gahe are notified of the plight of the Apache by Wind, who acts as messenger for them.

When the celebration was at its height two Gahe that no one had seen before appeared. They were beautifully decorated and their head-dresses were well designed. The Gahe that belonged to the Apache danced very well, but those two whom no one recognized danced much better; they were outstanding. The people asked one another about them. "Who owns these?" they asked.[1] No one knew.

When the Gahe stopped to rest and went back out of sight, these two also moved away from the fire. But they stopped far from the other Gahe and so the Gahe of the Apache learned nothing about them.

All of the Gahe danced till dawn. As dawn was breaking the two strangers went away somewhere. No one knew where they had gone. For four nights the two strangers kept coming. But still no one knew who they were or from whence they came because they always left while it was still dark.

Then the leading men said, "We must learn something about them. Tonight is the night to find out. We will learn where they go." They decided to saddle fast horses and to station men on them at intervals along the path those two usually took when they went away.

The fourth night the Gahe danced until the sun rose. The two strangers were still there. When they stopped dancing, the two strangers separated from the others and began to run toward the mountains. The riders were stationed at intervals along the way. The man on the fast-est horse was stationed nearest the mountains. The riders followed those Gahe. But the Gahe out-distanced the horses. Even the fastest horse could not keep up with them. These two Gahe ran toward a big mountain. When they reached it they stood in front of a sheer rock wall. Then they turned back toward the people and gave their call. The rock separated and they entered.

Then all the people gathered once more at the place where the cere-mony had been held. They did not like what they had done and dis-cussed it. They were frightened to think they had been chasing the true Gahe. "We have done something evil," they said. They urged the one who knew the ceremony of the Gahe to pray with all his power. "If we had not bothered them they might have done something good for us. We who are only men did wrong," they said.

Not long after that disease broke out among them and killed many of them.[2]

## B. WATER MONSTERS

### 1. *The Girl Who Married a Water Monster*

They say there are some springs in Mexico where Water Monster[3]

---

[1] That is, "Who has the right to decorate Gahe in this way?"

[2] The Gahe constitute the principal ritual defense of the Chiricahua in the face of an epidemic. It is noteworthy that widespread sickness is accordingly con-sidered the condign punishment for outraging these supernaturals.

[3] Water Beings, supernaturals who control the waters, are commonly en-countered in Apache mythology.

lives. Roger[1] tells a story about Water Monster. It happened close to Deming, New Mexico. There was a certain water hole there to which the Indians were afraid to go. It was said that something came out of the water at that place and grabbed people.

But once one girl, a girl of about sixteen years of age, went there to fill her water jar. She filled the jar, put a stopper of grass in, and then she disappeared. Her people missed her after a while and came to look for her. They found the jar and saw the marks made by her knees when she kneeled for the water.[2] Then they went back, for they thought she was dead.

But the old woman, her grandmother, stayed there and cried for four days. The fourth day something came to her and said, "The girl you are crying for is all right. She is living in a cave now. Go back and tell the people to pray and sing."

The old woman came back with this message. They held a big ceremony. They hired a powerful shaman and he said, "We shall sing for four nights."

The ceremony was held and the last night the power said, "Go to the pond and stay there. In the middle of the day something will rise."

The girl's father loved her. He did as he was directed. At the time mentioned a man came out of the water. He had long hair and his eye was as bright as a star. The girl was at his side.

She spoke to her father. "Father, I'm in a better country now. This is my husband. I can come back to you no more. But stay around these mountains all your life. I'll help you. I'll give you long life. All of your people will grow up and be happy. We'll help you out. No one shall harm you."

The man stayed there. He killed many deer there. Sometimes he would find a dead deer, still warm, killed for him.

But finally he went away and the Mexicans killed him. If he had done as his daughter told him he would not have lost his life.

### 2. *A Water Monster Story*

My father told me a story about a place called "Three Mountains"[3] near Deming, New Mexico, not far from the border of Old Mexico.

A woman went down to the spring there. Belle Nicholas' mother was there. My father was there too.[4] It was a very, very pretty girl who went. She was dressed in buckskin. They had told her, "Go to the spring

---

[1] The reference is to Roger Tolane, a Chiricahua Apache living at Mescalero, New Mexico.

[2] In another version a young man rises from the water and offers to fill her jar for her. When she hands the jar to him she is unable to let go and falls into the water. The jar is found floating on the surface of the water by her relatives.

[3] The Tres Hermanas Mountains.

[4] Despite the allusion to specific individuals we can be sure that this is a traditional story. It is found among different Apache tribes and is told in more than one version.

and get water." They waited for her. She didn't come back. The spring was just a little way from her camp. They went over to look for her after a while and found only the water jar. They discovered her trail and followed it. They saw she had walked to "Three Mountains." They didn't know where she was. They couldn't follow her any farther. They lived there a year and hunted all over for her. They had good shamans. They hired some who were good at finding lost objects to look for her. Finally they got the best one. He got all the people together. He sang and sang to find out where she was.

Then the singer said, "She's right there in 'Three Mountains'."

That was the place where this man had obtained his power. He told the people to come with him in that mountain. Belle's mother went there with him; my father, too, and others who were living in those days. He ordered those people who were going in there with him to cover themselves with pollen.

All at once, after they had worshipped at the rock wall, a place opened and a door appeared where there had not been one before. Bears and other fierce animals, the worst they had ever seen, were right there in front. But they worshipped just as the ceremonial man told them to do and they were all allowed to enter. Inside was a fine level bench of sand, very beautiful, and a big opening.

Those inside told them, "Go ahead, the leader is there. Go and see him."

They traveled ahead. They saw fierce animals but were not bothered.

The bear, the fierce animal, told them, "Your girl is married to the son of the power of this place. I don't believe she can leave this place even if she wants to. There is her camp." He pointed to a camp.

So they saw her in there. They urged her to go home with them. She was as pretty as could be and the man she had married in that holy cave was just as good-looking as she was. She didn't want to go back with her relatives. "I want to stay here. I don't want to go back to earth any more," she said.

The son-in-law said, "You people go back. But stay around this holy place. I'll watch you. You'll have plenty. Have no fear. Don't leave this region no matter how many enemies you see."

So they went out. The girl wouldn't go back with them. She also told them, "You stay around this holy place and you will increase in numbers. I'll be with you. You'll have plenty of horses and the enemy will not bother you."

But the people disobeyed. They went back to Arizona and the west. They all got killed. That's the way the old man used to tell it. The power of that place belonged to the father of the young man who married the girl. They don't say how the girl got in there, who led her into that place. It might have been Water Monster who took her there. When anything disappears at the water they suspect Water Monster.

### C. VISITS TO THE DEAD

### 1. *How the Antelope Got His Name*

I heard this story from a real old man many years ago when I was a boy. I didn't play so much like other boys. I used to stay where the old men were sitting around telling stories. All those things I know I heard from the old men who used to gather and talk at night. Once I asked an old man why the antelope has such a funny name, and he told me this story.

He said that one time a man fell in a battle. He was seriously wounded, was between life and death. When he was between life and death he started to go to "the place of reddish ground," the afterworld. That's what the old man called it. The man was already in that place, for he was more dead than alive. Unless he got out at once he would be there permanently, he knew; he would be dead. All at once he saw himself as this animal. He saw himself put on the nature of that animal, saw himself, his ghost, look as that animal looks today.

Then this animal dashed out of that place and got out on the plains. And this man, when this animal got out, came back to his senses, recovered, and did not die. Ever since then this animal has been called "he who is becoming," meaning that the man was becoming that animal.[1]

### 2. *The Woman Who Visited the Afterworld*[2]

In the place where the Chiricahua go after death, everything goes on as it did in the old days here. There is a sort of trap door with tall grass. When this opens a mountain of sand is there and you step on this and go down. You are not conducted there; it just opens. There is no particular place where this door is known to be.

Once at Fort Sill one old woman said a boy and girl appeared to her and said, "You are wanted in the other world." She went with them, went a little ways. The door opened and she slid down. The woman said that the same conditions as are found in this world prevail there. It was just as it is now and white people were down there. People were going to town. When she got down there others asked her what she wanted. She said that the children had told her to come along. The others scolded the children and explained that they were naughty and were always telling stories. She saw old people and children. Everyone kept the age

---

[1] The name is *zilahe* in the Chiricahua Apache language.

[2] This is a typical story of a visit to the underworld. The general pattern is as follows: A person who is very sick finds himself sliding down the mound of sand to the underworld. A relative guides him to the camps where his dead ancestors dwell. It is apparently not time for him to stay there and he is warned against eating food (usually fruit) offered to him. He refuses such nourishment and finds himself in the world above, recovering from the illness which has besieged him. He relates his adventure to those about him.

he was when he died. People who have experiences like this don't live long. This woman died shortly after this.[1]

The people down there are flesh and blood, just as we are. They play the hoop and pole game. If you go, as this woman did, and eat some food while you are down there, you can't come back. If you go down after death you cannot come back. Ghosts don't go right down though. They stay around the place where they died for a while; I don't know how long. There is no idea of punishment or reward in this afterworld and I don't know who has charge there.

### 3. *A Chiricahua Woman Visits the Underworld*[2]

A Chiricahua woman was very sick. Though they spoke to her she recognized nothing. Later she recovered her senses and got well. She said that her ghost had gone from her body and had come to a high bluff. Below there was darkness. Below she could see cottonwoods and a stream. She jumped off and landed on a great cone of sand. When she landed the sand began to move and she continued to go further down. Finally she reached the bottom and saw many camps. The people were living there just as we live here. It was light in that place.

She started to go toward the camps and recognized some of her relatives there. Two of her youngest relatives met her and were happy to see her. All the people she met looked as they had in life and she could see no difference between life down there and life here. Her relatives led her to the camps and she came to her father and mother. On the way her two relatives warned her not to accept food at her father's camp if she wished to get back to earth again.

She followed this advice. Her relatives were happy to see her again and prepared food, but she refused to eat. This woman had had two husbands and when they saw her they started to come to her and fought over her. Her two younger relatives seemed to be protecting her through all this. They advised her to go back to earth and told her how to do so. Her ghost came back to her body and she opened her eyes.

[1] To think or dream of death is an ill omen, presaging one's own imminent fate; to have such an experience as the one recounted here is even more serious.

[2] For an explanation of the psychological and social implications of such stories as these see Opler "An Interpretation of Ambivalence of Two American Indian Tribes," *Journal of Social Psychology*, Vol. 7, 1936, 82–116, and "Further Comparative Anthropological Data Bearing on the Solution of a Psychological Problem," *Journal of Social Psychology*, Vol. 9, 1938, 477–483.

# V. STORIES OF FOOLISH PEOPLE, UNFAITH-FULNESS, AND PERVERSION

## A. THE FOOLISH PEOPLE

### 1. *The Foolish People Obtain a Horse*

There were some foolish people living at Head Springs and over that way from the Agency buildings in the old days. I think they must have been the first people in this region.[1] They must have been some kind of Apache because their language was nearly like Mescalero. Out towards Head Springs you can see where they used to scrape some of those old pines on the side.[2] There are many stories about these people and about how silly they were. They were living here when the Mescalero were in the region, but it seems they died off very quickly. They went almost naked, wearing just a little hide. They had no houses. They didn't even know how to get on a horse.

One of the stories is about a Mescalero who was married to one of these people. He brought his horse to the place where they were camped. These people were so foolish that they wondered what the horse could eat. They didn't even know what to call the horse so they had a council to talk it over. First they tried to feed the horse gravy, but the horse wouldn't eat that. Then they tried coffee. They tried everything they had. That Mescalero just stood there and nearly died laughing. Finally he staked the horse out and let it eat grass. Then they all said, "Look! It must be grass that that animal eats!"

Then they wanted to know how to ride that horse. One got on but he sat facing the horse's tail. Finally the Mescalero got on the right way and rode all over. Those silly people said he must have pitch on his buttocks to stick there.

### 2. *The Foolish Men Call like Crows*

One of these foolish people called a big council. They agreed that they would break up the council just about dark and each man would go home and have intercourse with his wife. They were to do this when they heard the sound of a crow and each man was to make this souud as he got home and did it.

They broke up the council and every man hurried for his camp. Some hadn't even got back to their camps when the crowing started. And pretty soon all you heard was crowing.

[1] Other Apache groups, including the Jicarilla and Lipan tell similar "foolish people" stories. Therefore it is very unlikely that these stories refer to a definitely localized group as the informant would have us believe.

[2] The Mescalero formerly used the sweet inner coating of pine bark for food and were doubtless responsible for the condition of these trees.

### 3. *A Foolish Man Loses His Parfleche*

A whole bunch of these foolish people were going along. Finally they made camp and one man camped on the side of a hill where there was a steep bluff below. He put down his parfleche there and went off. While he was gone it rolled down the hill and dropped off this bluff. Pretty soon the man came back. He looked around for his parfleche. It was gone.

He called, "Everybody come here!"

They came and had a big council there. Finally they decided that they'd trail that parfleche. But they just trailed it to the edge of the bluff. They didn't have sense enough to look over the edge and see it down there. A Mescalero Indian was there and told the story. It shows how silly they were.

### 4. *The Foolish Men Go on a Raid*

One time these poeple went out on the war-path. Some men wanted to go out on a raid and get something valuable, so they just started out. They had no guns or anything. While they were going along one man found an old piece of cowhide which had been used to hobble a horse. He thought he had done something great. He acted as if he had found a fortune. And so he turned back and wouldn't go on any farther.

### 5. *Two Foolish Men Escape from the Comanche*

Another story tells how two of these people got away from some Comanche. They had built a little fire to cook rabbits. Some Comanche had come from Oklahoma and were crawling up on them to kill them. One of these foolish men began to throw the rabbit gut over his head and out into the brush. A piece of it hit the Comanche chief. He thought this was such a silly thing to do that he began to laugh. This warned the two foolish men and they got away.

The one good thing they say about these people is that they were very fast runners. They were faster than horses even. The soldiers and the cowboys couldn't catch them.

### 6. *The Foolish People Are Shot by the Soldiers*[1]

Once these foolish people had a big camp. The soldiers came and commenced to shoot at them. Instead of running away they stood right there and began to talk to each other. They said, "Why are these people shooting us?" And they began to try to get the soldiers to stop it. But their talking did no good and most of them got killed. Finally one old man advised them to run and the few that were left got away.

---

[1] As can be readily understood, many of these stories serve a didactic function. Excessive trust in outsiders is ridiculed in this particular tale.

## 7. The Adventures of the Foolish People on a Raid[1]

One time these foolish people went south to try to steal horses and cattle. They left their women in a hiding place in the mountain.[2] On their way they came upon a horse.

"What is this?" they asked one another. Not one of them knew.

One said, "I see it carries four rocks." He was referring to its hooves. "These are holy rocks," he said.

Then they wondered what it ate. They offered it many things, but it wouldn't eat them. Finally they turned it loose and found out that it eats grass.

They went on. Three were walking together. A grasshopper flew up and lit on the forehead of one of these men. He said to another, "Shoot it! Shoot it!" He thought only the grasshopper would be killed. The man shot and killed his friend.

They were carrying bundles of food. They stopped near a cliff. One man's bundle rolled down and off the cliff while he was away. When he came back he looked for it. He trailed it to the edge of the cliff. He could have seen it below if he had looked down, but he didn't have sense enough to look over the cliff and so couldn't find it.

When they were about to steal horses the Mexicans came after them. They just stood there. They told the Mexicans to stop, but the Mexicans just kept on killing these foolish people.

"Why are they killing us?" one asked another.

When only a few were left one yelled, "Let's get away or they'll kill us all."

A few got away, but most of them were killed. That's why they didn't last.

They started back home. Just before they got home one said, "It's sundown now. As soon as we get home, the first one on his wife must make a noise like a crow."

When they got to the camp each man ran for his dwelling, and as they began to do it, you heard the voice of the crow from all directions.

Now the Chiricahua laugh about it. As a joke they say, "When we get home we'll act like Crow."[3]

---

[1] A different informant from the one who told the preceding Foolish People stories tells this tale. While some of the episodes are a repetition, new motifs are introduced too.

[2] This was the usual practice while the men were away on some dangerous errand.

[3] For a Chiricahua Foolish People tale which does not appear here see Hoijer, *op. cit.*, pp. 37–38, "The Foolish People Acquire Coffee." In this story the Foolish People try to soften coffee by boiling the beans, until a Mescalero teaches them how to use it correctly.

## B. Unfaithfulness

### 1. The Woman Who Pretended Sickness and Death To Be with Her Lover

A certain married woman a long time ago wanted another man, and, instead of divorcing her husband, pretended she was dead. They buried her in a grave with brush on top. She had arranged with her lover to have him pull her out. This man took her out and they lived out on the edge of camp where no one could see them.

One day the woman came to a watering place and saw her children. She was glad to see them and held them on her lap.

Later they told their father, but he said, "Don't talk like that."[1]

It happened twice. The father got suspicious. He went there himself and looked and found them together. He shot them both. He told the rest of the people that he had killed two animals over there.[2]

### 2. The Unfaithful Wife Found Out by Her Husband

A certain woman acted as though she were very sick. She told her husband, "I don't feel well with so many people around. I will be better if we live on a quiet ridge."

He moved the camp away. The woman hobbled off every morning with the aid of a cane.

One day her husband saw her without the cane talking to a young man. Then he saw her with her arms around the man. The next day he watched. She met the same man. That day she came home limping. When she pushed aside the cowhide at the entrance to come in the wickiup, he hit her with a club.

Then he said to her, "You are going to dance naked before all the camp to show that you're not lame, or I am going to kill you. If you decide to dance that way before every camp, then I'll let you marry that man. If you don't marry that man after you dance, I'll kill you anyway."

### 3. The Woman Who Pretended Sickness To Be with Her Lover

This happened a long time ago. There was a young woman living with her husband, but they had no children. She fell in love with another man. She wanted to marry him, but her husband was in the way, you see. Finally she started to play sick. Her father, mother, and a brother lived close by. They all noticed that she didn't eat much. She tied a cloth on her chest, and she got quite thin.

One day her husband thought he would go out hunting and get meat for her. By this time she was walking with a cane. They all felt sorry,

---

[1] Because the dead should not be mentioned.

[2] It was the rule that a man who discovered his wife to be unfaithful could punish her and her lover as he saw fit without expectation of vengeance from the relatives of either.

for she was a pretty woman too. Her husband told her, "You stay with
your mother and father, and tomorrow I'll go out and kill deer." He
said this at night, and she replied, "All right."

He left before daybreak. As soon as her husband went away, instead
of going to her parents, she went into the woods towards the river.
Some people were watching her. When she got a little ways she left her
cane under some leaves and walked on as well as ever. She looked for
her lover along the river bank and found him. She stayed in the brush
all day with that man. About sundown she came out and started back
to her camp. She tied the cloth around her chest again, found the stick,
and walked slowly to her camp. When her husband came back she was
in bed playing sick. She told her husband to cook meat for her. He
cooked it and fed her.

The next day her husband left again. She watched him go. She followed him and saw that he had gone to the place where the men play
hoop and pole. She went back to her camp and then started to the river
again. She found her lover and stayed with him all day. At sundown
she came home again. Others watched her. They saw her leave the
stick and cloth by a tree.

As the husband was coming home he met a man who asked him,
"Where were you today?"

He answered, "Playing hoop and pole."

"Where's your wife?"

"At home, sick,"

"I'll tell you something if you won't tell on me."

"All right."

Then he told him. He said, "One of my boys was out shooting birds
in the brush today and saw your wife with a man."

In those days they often killed a woman and a man for doing that.
They cut the nose sometimes, too, for it.[1]

The woman hobbled home slowly again. She went to bed. When her
husband came she asked for something to eat. He cooked for himself.
She asked for some. Finally he gave her some. Then she asked for water
and he gave her some. He never said anything to her.

The next morning the man cooked meat for breakfast. He fed her and
said, "I'm going to the hoop and pole game. You go to your people.[2]
I'll come there and then you can come home with me."

He started off. He went a little way, and then he fooled her; he turned
around and got back to his camp. She was already gone. He went to
the neighbors and asked where she was. They said that she had gone
to the river and told him to go back to his family. But he said "No."

He went to his tipi and got his bow and arrows. He went to the river
and looked through the reeds. There under the bank by the reeds she

---

[1] As this passage indicates, the cutting off of the tip of an unfaithful wife's
nose was a possible punishment among the Chiricahua.

[2] Note the assumption of matrilocal residence, the assumption that the relatives of the woman live close by.

was lying with the man. He came down to the bank and crawled close to them. He shot the man through the side first. Then he shot the woman through the chest. He left them together as they lay.

He went back to the hoop and pole grounds. He said to the men there, "I just killed a female mountain-lion and a male mountain-lion down by the river."

They liked the hide for quivers in those days and so they all ran down. And they found the bodies.

They didn't do anything to the husband. It was their law then.

## C. PERVERSION

### 1. *The Woman Who Abused Herself with Cactus*

A long time ago there was a pretty young woman living with her husband. They had no children. When her husband was away she would go up the mountain side. Half way up there was thick brush. People saw her go there, and her husband, too, noticed that when he came to camp unexpectedly she wasn't around.

For a long time he didn't say anything. Then once, after leaving camp, he turned around and came back. She was going up there and he followed her. He saw her go into the thicket. From a distance he could see that she was sitting on something and wiggling around. Then she would get up, look down, and shake her dress. After a while she went back to camp.

After that he went to that place and saw what it was. There were two low cacti there. The thorns had been taken off and the outer skin shaved off until they were the right size. The man took his knife and cut both of them close to the ground, leaving just enough uncut to hold them there. He went back to camp and never said anything to her.

The next afternoon he went off again, and she started for the brush. She began to do the same thing, but when she got it in the cactus broke off. She tried to get it out, but it went in farther; she couldn't get it out. She came home. She told her husband she was sick, but she wouldn't tell what was the matter. Still her husband said nothing about it.

But she couldn't urinate and began to swell up. She nearly died, and she finally had to tell. Her husband got an old man to come to her. This man shot little barbed arrows in there and was able to pull the cactus out with these. When the cactus came out, the water squirted and went all over the old man.

Then the husband said to her, "I was going to kill you, but you have suffered enough. I'll just send you away. Go where I won't see you again."

## D. FOOLISH OLD MEN

### 1. *The Foolish Old Men*

There were two old men there. The people did not like them because they did not take care of themselves. They went without clothes. They followed the people and were always behind. The people went back to look for them and found them carrying a big bundle of carrizo. The old men stopped when the group stopped, went into a cave, and built a fire. Some men from the camps went to spy on them. The two old men were lying on their sides with their heads in opposite directions. They had nothing on. One of the spies took a bundle of carrizo. The spy heated a stick and burned the buttocks of one of the old men. The two old men didn't see him but got mad at each other. Then they went to sleep again. The spy did the same thing to the other man. Then they started to fight.[1]

The other people from the camp went on. The people killed a horse and butchered it, built a fire, and put ribs on each side of the fire. Then the two old men came and picked up the meat. One of the old men had a bone inside of which there was marrow. He wanted the marrow. He held the bone behind him and went over to the people. He asked them how they got the marrow out of the bones, if they had a rock to break it with. They said, "You just hit that man on the head. That is the way we get the marrow out." So he went over and hit the man on the head. The marrow came out and the man was killed.

They all went away. They disliked the old fellows more. They wanted to get rid of them but did not want to kill them. They camped at another place. The two old men were there. The people said, "Let's look for a steep place. Maybe we can do something with them." They found such a place. They all left the camp, went to the steep place with the old men following them. One man told the people to make a path straight up the steep place. They put a big rock there. They made a path to the edge of the steep place and right down to the bottom. They started on the edge of the steep hill and came down on the other side. The two men came to the edge of the steep place and looked for tracks because there was a path. Then they saw the people at the bottom. So they held hands and started down. They fell down. One fell on his head at the bottom and knocked his brains out there. The other was saved. He started to eat the brain. He was talking to the dead man. "Get up and eat this good brain!"

[1] A trick played on two old persons (sometimes a man and wife) which instigates a quarrel between them, is a common Apache myth element. Usually Coyote is the miscreant, however.

# VI. MISCELLANEOUS

## 1. *Why Grease Is Rubbed on the Legs*

In the old days the men used to get a lot of fat meat. They were feeding their stomachs and getting very fat. One man wouldn't put fat on his legs or face. All the other men put it on their legs, saying, "I'm going to feed you; let me be a good runner."

This man who wouldn't ever do it or worship got fat in the belly. Then the enemy came and all the others ran away and got to safety. But this man couldn't run. Then his legs told him, "You never fed us when you had good fat meat. Now run with your belly."

That's how the thing started, I guess. It's a true story, they say. Because this happened, in my time and long before that, the Chiricahua have taught their children to feed their legs. I guess the girls do it too. Even in these days the Chiricahua never neglect it. If a man has just a little fat on his hands, he rubs it on his legs. I do it myself many times.

## 2. *The Lazy Boy Who Became a Great Runner*[1]

There was a boy a long time ago who everybody thought was very lazy. He was too lazy to eat even. He would lie down all day long. The other boys were out playing, but he never joined them. He wet his bed all the time too because he was too lazy to get up.

Finally they began to wonder about him. He seemed to be gone all night, and he came in at daybreak and slept all day. As soon as it was dark he went again. They didn't know where he went or what he did.

One day his family was hungry. They had used up all their provisions and there was nothing to eat. The boy had no weapon, nothing to kill deer with, but he went out and ran down a deer on foot. This was in the daytime. After that he did it often. He would catch wild antelopes on foot too.

Then they found out what he had been doing those nights. He had been practicing running, and he got to be a great runner.

## 3. *The Boy Who Tamed an Eagle and Trained It to Hunt*

A young boy climbed up a cliff and reached an eagle's nest. He brought down one of the eaglets. He took it home with him.

People said to him, "Throw it away! It will make you sick!"[2] But he didn't.

---

[1] This is a very sketchy account of a story which becomes greatly elaborated in the versions obtained from other Apache groups. See Opler, *Dirty Boy: A Jicarilla Tale of Raid and War*, Memoir of the American Anthropological Association, No. 52, 1938.

[2] Because eagles eat snakes, from which the Chiricahua believe a sickness can be contracted, and are therefore unclean.

91

He kept it and fed it and raised it. It became his friend. Wherever he went, the eagle went with him. It flew along by his side. When he saw a deer he told the eagle to get it, and the eagle would catch it for him. The eagle would bring him a rabbit or anything he wanted.

## 4. *The Magic Ring*[1]

Long, long ago when the birds and animals could talk, there was an old Indian woman who had a grandson fifteen or sixteen years of age. They were the only two Indians around there.

They were very hungry and poor, so they came and stayed at the edge of a town. After a while the woman went into the town. There she saw a woman washing clothes and she asked this woman for some work. The woman hired her to wash for a small sum a day.

When she got back to the boy later in the day they built themselves a little dwelling. She gave the money she had earned to her grandson. The next day she went out to work again. She brought back her pay, gave it to the boy, and told him to get bread and coffee with it.

So the boy started for town. He came to a store and went in. There was no one present to sell him anything. He waited there. Then a little dog jumped on the counter and asked, "What do you want?"

The boy said, "Where is the man? I want to buy bread."

"Buy me," said the puppy.

Just then the man came in and asked the boy what he wanted. And the boy bought the dog for half his money.

When he got home his grandmother asked him where the bread was and he had to tell her that he had bought the dog instead. The old woman was very angry but she said nothing to him.

The next day when the old woman was going out to work she told the boy to buy bread with the rest of the money. He started for the store once more. The same thing happened. Another puppy was there and told the boy to buy him. When the storekeeper came in, the boy offered to pay out the rest of his money for the dog. The man laughed and sold him the puppy. Now he had two of them.

The puppies grew rapidly and became big dogs. The boy stayed with them while his grandmother worked in town.

One day the first dog told him, "Go over to the town. Ask for the man who has charge of the roads. He will ask you what you want. Then say to him, 'Did you lose anything that you loved even better than yourself?' He has lost his son and we will help you bring him back to

---

[1] This tale is obviously of European origin. It doubtless reached the Chiricahua Apache through their contact with Mexican villagers. The story was obtained from an Eastern Chiricahua (Warm Springs Apache), a member of the band of the Chiricahua which had the earliest peaceful contact with the Mexicans. Dr. Parsons has called attention to the resemblance between this story and the familiar European tale sometimes referred to as "The Helpful Animals."

life. The father will offer you many things for this, but ask for nothing more than the ring he wears."

So the boy went to this man and asked him whether he had lost something very precious to him. "I will give it back to you if you will pay me well," he told him.

"No, I have lost nothing."

"Think."

"Well, I lost my son two years ago, but you can't bring the dead to life."

"Yes, that's what I mean. I can do it. But what will you pay me?"

This man had many things. He had stores and cattle. He said, "I'll give you a store."

"No."

"I'll give you all three of my stores."

"No."

"I'll give you cattle too."

"No, I want nothing but that gold ring on your finger."

"Why, that's nothing! I'll give you the stores and other things in addition."

"I'll take the ring only."

The boy went out. In a little while he came back with the son of this man. The man gave him the ring at once but when he gave it he told the boy, "Be very careful and do not lose this ring."

The boy brought the ring home. He and his grandmother were poor and ragged. They didn't know what good the ring would do them. But the dogs told him, "Brother, tonight when you go to bed put the ring under your pillow. When you wake up you will have houses and riches and your grandmother will be a young girl of sixteen or seventeen."

And that is exactly what happened. He put the ring under his pillow the second night and in the morning he had the best negro cook and everything was ready and cooking.

The principal man of the town had a beautiful daughter that the boy wanted for his wife. He told the ring about it and put the ring under his pillow the third night. When he woke up the girl was lying at his side. He kept on that way. He got everything he wanted.

But the girl did not like him very well. One day she found out how he got all these things. That night when he was asleep she took the ring and put it under her own pillow. "When I wake up let me be on an island in the ocean with everything I want, and let the boy be in the same place where he was before he got the ring."

In the morning the boy was back in his grass hut and the girl was in a fine place out on an island.

The man from whom the boy had got the ring heard that the boy was poor once more. He knew at once that the boy must have lost the ring. He came to the boy and the boy had to admit it. Then he told the boy, "You must have that ring found within four days or I'm going to drown you. I'm going to put you in an iron pot and put the pot in a place where the water flows. The water comes in just fast enough so that it can be pumped out by hand. You'll be fastened in there and will have to pump for your life. If the ring is not there in four days I'll let the water flow faster and you'll die."

The boy cried and told the dogs. He told the dogs to go all over and find the girl and the ring. The man put the boy in the pot and he had to pump for his life.

The grandmother gave the dogs food and they started out. That night they returned puffing. They had been far, but they had seen no trace of the girl. They came to the boy in the pot. He told them to go out again. So the next day they started out again. At night they returned. They had found nothing. The boy told them to try again, so the third morning they went out. For the third time they were unsuccessful. When they came back at sundown the boy was still in the pot. He was all tired out and ready to give up. But the dogs told him they would try again.

So the fourth day they started for the ocean. "We've been all over now but we've never been there," one said to the other. They came to the seashore. There the frogs were soldiers. They went to the officer and asked him about the ring and the girl. The officer knew nothing about it but he called the bugle boy and had him call for the soldiers. As soon as the bugle blew the frog soldiers came and formed in line. The officer asked each one if lately he had seen a house somewhere where he had never seen one before. Finally he came to one soldier who said, "Yes, I saw a fine house on an island where I never saw one before."

The dogs asked the officer whether this man could take them to that place, and the frog soldiers went over with them.

It was nearly sundown when they got there. On the island there was a big house and it looked new. On this island were many mouse soldiers. The dogs asked the mouse officer about the house. He said the house was new all right. He had the bugle blown and the soldiers lined up. None knew how the house had come to be there. None could tell who lived there either. So the soldiers surrounded the house. But it was locked up and they could not get in.

While they were trying to get in some ants came along. The ants, when they heard what they were doing, agreed to help them. So the ants crawled in through the keyhole, unlocked the door and let the mice and frogs in.

The girl was in there asleep. They looked all over, under the pillow, under the bed, and everywhere. But they could not find the ring. First they thought it must be in her mouth. Then one said, "I'll bet she has it in her rectum."

They had some chili powder with them. One mouse put his tail in it and then drew it across the girl's nose. Meanwhile the ants went under the cover and waited. When the chili powder came close to her nose, the girl sneezed and the ring came out of her rectum. The ants grabbed it and handed it to the mice. They gave it to the frogs. The frogs gave it to the dogs, and the dogs hurried across the ocean.

It was just about sunset now, the end of the last day. The boy had given up hope already. Then, just in time, the dogs appeared with the ring. The man had to turn the boy loose again.

### 5. *The Quarrel between Wind and Lightning*

Lightning and Wind got into an argument as to who did the most good and was most powerful. Lightning told Wind that he was most powerful. "You can't do the things I can." Wind got angry and hid from the earth. They looked for him. They hired all the hawks and other birds to look for him. They were having too little rain. They hired the black and yellow bee too, for he can go into small crevices.

At last they found Wind in a far region. Bee found him there. A continuous odor of grass came from the place where he sat and the vicinity. The bees could not approach because of it. The bees went on the four directions. They kept in the air. All at once the wind saw them before him.

Wind spoke to them. He said, "You must have got help from some supernatural being, for no one can approach me in this manner."

The bees called the name of the wind, for it was an emergency, and they called his name to his face.[1] "Wind," they called, "you are wanted back. The people are suffering. It is your duty to come back and do your work."

"But the lightning said he could do without me. That is why I left. How is it that you people want me back now? I have many things to say to Lightning, but I guess I'll just send him about four messages. I'll be at a certain mountain top and Lightning can wait for me on a rainbow and I will speak to him. Four days after you go I will be there."

On the fourth day Sun was there and Lightning and Earth were there too. Sun came from the east in the form of a little cyclone. Wind and Thunder[2] embraced.

Lightning said, "We've been wondering where you've been."

Wind replied, "You said you were more powerful; that is why I went away. Why is it that the earth is so hot that it is about to burn up?"

The breathing of the thunder created four persons and these were sent out in the four directions, and they were told that whenever the earth trembles they should come to the center. Lightning and Wind used that power to make the earth as it was before, with green grass and the proper amount of water. Sun had a pipe for them. They smoked

---

[1] The personal name of a Chiricahua Apache is not called in his presence unless an emergency exists or a plea of some kind is to be made to him.

[2] Thunder is here used as a synonym for lightning by the informant since these two are considered aspects of the same force often in ceremonial contexts.

and agreed to have no more trouble after that. At this conference the seasons were made.

## 6(a). Herus and Kantaneiro

A long time ago a man named Herus[1] came among the Apache. The people did not know from where he came. He had a book. When he was becoming old he told them that he would leave them this book. He directed them to keep it and to pass it from family to family. But they didn't believe him. After he was gone they burned the book.[2] Then they were lost.

Later Kantaneiro[3] came. This was still before the whites came from across the ocean. He was a great fighter. He always carried a spear only. Once the Mexicans came. The Indians ran away. He stayed and drove the Mexicans off with nothing but his loin cloth. With this he hit them and he killed the officers. They shot at him, but he couldn't be hit.

Kantaneiro had a book too. He directed them to keep it as Herus had done. But again they did not obey. When he died they burned it.

These two were prophets from heaven, like John Baptist or Moses.

## 6(b). Herus (Variant)

At the beginning a man, Herus, was given a book by Yusn and Child-of-the-Water. There were many Indians then. In this big book it told of things from the beginning to the end. The man who was given the book could not read, but when he opened it he could understand it. Herus had children and a wife. He told his children to carry the book after his death. "Then only old age will kill you."

This man died of old age. At his death they burned everything and killed horses, and the book was burned too. Herus had told them, "There will be white people, and if you have the book you will be over the white people. But if you lose it you will be lower and know nothing."

When Herus died they moved the camp. They heard a voice. There in the sky was Herus. He said, "Why are you crying? I am in a good place, in my father's home. We will meet again." Herus said, "When a person of old age dies, he will be a boy in heaven. If you keep in mind what I told you of the book, you will enter the kingdom of God and have everlasting life."

[1] The word Herus is undoubtedly the Apache version of Jesus as the name first came to them from Spanish sources. The Chiricahua do not associate the term with Jesus, who has been associated instead with the culture hero, Child-of-the-Water.

[2] The book was burned in obedience to the rule which demands that all of a dead person's possessions be destroyed.

[3] Kantaneiro is most likely a familiar Biblical or early Spanish character. The writer has been unable to place the name with certainty, however. The name is variously rendered and translated. A number of characteristics have been attributed to this figure, who seems highly unstable in Chiricahua mythology. By some it is said that he inaugurated prayer at the mounds of stones which act as wayside shrines.

When you put anything away that you like and you are afraid for it, this belongs to Herus, and it will be safe.

Herus said, "There aren't white people, but there will be white people, and Yusn who made us is pitying us, and we don't know anything. He will turn you over to the white people and let them teach you. They will come from the east. I have spoken to you often from the book, but now that I have left you, you are going to be slaves for the people coming. These people are coming from across the ocean. Call them "grey-eyed enemies." They will take your country but will teach you. So when these people come, because you burned the book, they will capture you and send you east.[1] I can't help you. When you start as captives to the east, you will be all scattered. By the time you return to your mountains, there will be only a few Indians, like grain leaking from a sack. But there will be a few others here of another language. When you get back there will be many white people here in your country, and they will argue over killing the Indians and have a war just over the Indians. You will go through all this trouble, but I can't help you as this is the way Yusn gives his orders. There will be many whites, but since they have scattered the Indians, they will war among themselves until they are of an equal number to the Indians, and then Yusn will give us eternal life. Seven days before the war you will know. When I was with you I was Herus; now I am Yusn. So, my friends and my children, I want you to pray to Child-of-the-Water and Yusn, and after you believe in him you will have everlasting life. You can pray to me and to Child-of-the-Water and be prepared to receive me night or day. There are other people of different colors and different languages, but you are all my children, and I will have bears and other animals on this earth. There will be food for all.

At that time we were shown the herbs and their use for sickness. He said to pray for the herbs before giving them and to sing while giving them. "The white people will have their medicine, and the Indians too," we were told.

"After all these things happen, from then on there will be no more sickness, but everlasting life, so think of me. Your soul and that with which you think are mine."

At this place the cloud appeared over the dwelling, and he told them all this.[2]

---

[1] This is a retrospective rationalization of the captivity of the Chiricahua in the east following the Indian War of 1886.

[2] Another Chiricahua gave the same story in outline without naming the central figure. His account follows:

"Life Giver gave a certain Indian a book. As long as that book was kept the Indians would prosper. If it were destroyed, many troubles, such as a decrease in population, would befall them. When this man died, the Indians destroyed the book with the rest of this man's possessions, according to Indian custom. Therefore bad luck came to them."

The narrator, a thoughtful young Indian who is an active enough participant

## 7. *The Origin of Old Age*

One man was very old. He had been able to run like a horse but he could do so no longer. He was wondering why. He sat on a mountain side and thought his life over. He looked at his hair. It was beginning to get gray. His skin was different. He didn't know what age was, but he could tell that there was a difference. It worried him.

Finally something told him, "If you are worrying about this getting old, go to the ocean and dive in without shutting your eyes. Keep them open till you come up. If you do this you will feel young again. If you close your eyes you are going to get old."

He went south to the Gulf. When he got there he took off his clothes and jumped in. The water was salty and he couldn't keep his eyes open. The first thing you know he had to shut them. When he came out he blinked and blinked.

After that he got older and older. And since then people get old. If that man had done as he was told, he would have kept youth for us. We'd all be young all the time.

There was also a woman who didn't know what age was. She, too, felt queer. Her eyes, everything, felt different.

"Prepare some food to take with you," her supernatural power told her, "and go on a journey. Go without stopping until you pass over four white mountains. Go to the other side of the fourth mountain. If you stop before this you will get old."

She started to the east, carrying food. She went a long way and reached the first mountain. The mountain was steep. She went up and down it. She went a little way on the other side and she came to the second mountain. Again she went up it and down. Then she came to the third mountain. She went half way up the third mountain and she got very tired and hungry. She stopped and sat down and ate and rested. So she got age for us too. She kept getting older and older.

Supernatural Power talked to another man. It said "I'm going to tell you something that is hard to do. If you try you can do it though. You are getting to middle age now, but I can show you how you can become like a young boy again."

This man listened. The power said, "Start from here. Go back to the place where you first began to walk as a child. Then trail yourself through all the places you have been since you were a child. If you do not miss a place, the day you finish you will be young again and stay that way always."

---

in white culture to be comparatively and critically minded, made this comment on his story: "I do not think this is an old Indian idea. I think such stories as these were made up by the missionaries long ago and told to the Indians to illustrate certain things, and to make things easier for the Indian to understand. These stories have been taken over by the Indian and mixed with Indian ideas as they are retold. The book is probably the Bible, and the reason the story was told was to get the Indians to hang on to the Bible."

(a) A girl has a tame eagle which attacks a boy who tries to visit her at night.

(b) Beaver marries Piñon Jay. The children have the backs of beavers instead of bird tails and go to live in the water.

(c) At Hot Springs there is a high bluff and a canyon beyond it. White-Painted Woman crosses this canyon on a strand of spider "rope" which Spider stretches over it.

(d) A man wounds a deer but loses it. While he is looking for its tracks he meets Eagle. Eagle dresses him in a suit of eagle feathers and takes him on a flight to the other side of the sky. This is a disjointed version of a myth that assumes real importance for the Jicarilla and Navaho. It is probably a recent acquisition of the Chiricahua, and seems to be unknown to most of them.

(e) The ants were once people. When they were people they spoke the Navaho language, so they must be Navaho. There was a song they sang when they were people. It was about the black rocks, the Malpais, and told that this was their home. (Cf. footnote 1, p. 69.)

# APPENDIX

## COMPARATIVE NOTES ON CHIRICAHUA APACHE MYTHOLOGY

### By DAVID FRENCH

THE COMPARATIVE references in this appendix show the distribution of Chiricahua stories and incidents among the Southern Athabaskan, or Apachean-speaking, peoples.[1] The notes are arranged so as to parallel the stories in the body of this volume; the order of presentation and the numbering system are the same.

The references are given by tribe, author, and page. In the bibliography, where the sources are listed, there are cases where several works follow an author's name. This makes it necessary to examine the titles to discover the publication on the mythology of a particular tribe.

### KEY TO ABBREVIATIONS

| | |
|---|---|
| CHIR | Chiricahua Apache |
| Fran. F. | The Franciscan Fathers |
| Gd. | Pliny Earle Goddard |
| Gn. | Grenville Goodwin |
| Hoij. | Harry Hoijer |
| JIC | Jicarilla Apache |
| LIPAN | Lipan Apache |
| Matth. | Washington Matthews |
| MESC | Mescalero Apache |
| NAV | Navaho |
| Op. | Morris Edward Opler |
| Reich. | Gladys A. Reichard |
| Russ. | Frank Russell |
| S. CARLOS | San Carlos Apache |
| WHITE MT | White Mountain Apache |

*Story
Number*

IA1a. *Flood—Biblical type*          CHIR: Op., 1, 2.
LIPAN: Op., 10, 10(?). JIC: Op., 111–13, (note 1) 111. NAV:
Fran. F., 360–61(?); Stephen (b), 92–95(?). WESTERN APACHE
(Tribe undesignated): Curtis, 27–28. WHITE MT: Gn., 50–51.
S. CARLOS: Gd., 8, 28–29. Although these myths differ appre-

---

[1] While these notes have been especially compiled to accompany the preceding collection of mythology, they are ultimately based on a year's research made possible by a grant from the American Council of Learned Societies.

ciably from each other, they have been classed together because
they all possess at least some elements of the European "Noah's
Flood" story. The other Apachean accounts of floods and *Primeval water* seem to be aboriginal.

IA1b. *Flood—Biblical type* (See IA1a.)
    *Choice of culture types*          CHIR: Hoij., 13–14; Op., 2.
WESTERN APACHE (Tribe undesignated): Bourke, 210, 211–
12. WHITE MT: Gd., 118; Gn., 8–9, 19–20. Compare IB2.
*Origin of food types.*

IB1a. *Origin of culture hero(es)—supernatural conception*    CHIR: Hoij.,
    5–6; Op., 2–3, 5.
MESC: Hoij., 183; Op., ms. LIPAN: Op., 16, 22–23. JIC:
Mooney, 200–01; Russ., 255; Curtis, 62; Op., 48–49. NAV:
Packard, 85; Matth. (a), 215–16; Stevenson, (Cp. 279); Van
Vleet, 72–73, 73; Matth. (e), 105–06; Curtis, 98; Fran. F., 359–
60; Buxton, 297; Gd., (Cp. 140, 142), 153–55; Haile, 91–93;
Newcomb and Reich., 25–26; Reich., 38. WESTERN APACHE
(Tribe undesignated): Bourke, 210. WHITE MT: Gd., 93, 115–
16, 120; Gn., 3–4, 16–18. S. CARLOS: Gd., 8, 30–31.
    *Trick—crying explained*               CHIR: Op., 4.
    *Trick—excrement explained*         CHIR: Hoij., 6, Op., 4.
MESC: Hoij., 183.
    *Trick—tracks explained*           CHIR: Hoij., 6; Op., 4–5.
MESC: Hoij., 183–84; Op., ms. NAV: Matth. (e), 108.
    *Killing of giant*           CHIR: Hoij., 6–9; Op., 5–7, 13–14.
MESC: Hoij., 184–85; Op., ms. LIPAN: Op., (Cp. 35). NAV:
Matth. (a), 218–19; Van Vleet, 77–78; Matth. (e), 114–16; Curtis,
105; Buxton, 301–02; Haile, 109–13; Newcomb and Reich., 29–
30. WHITE MT: Gn., 10, 10–12, 23–24.
    *Killing of monster eagles*    CHIR: Hoij., 10–12; Op., 8–9, 12–13, 99.
MESC: Hoij., 186–87; Op., ms. LIPAN: Op., 19–20. JIC:
Mooney, 205–08; Russ., 257–58; Curtis, 66–68; Gd., 198–99;
Op., 61–65. NAV: Matth. (a), 220–22; Matth. (e), 118–21; Haile,
117–23; Newcomb and Reich., (Cp. 30–31). WHITE MT: Gn.,
13–16, 20–21; S. CARLOS: Gd., 16–19, 40–41.
    *Killing of monster from underground* CHIR: Hoij., 9–10; Op., 9–10.
MESC: Hoij., 185–86; Op., ms. LIPAN: Op., 17–18. JIC:
Mooney, 204–05; Russ., 255–57; Curtis, 65–66; Gd., 197–98;
Op., 58–61. NAV: Matth. (a), 219–20; Matth. (e), 116–18; Haile,
113–17; Newcomb and Reich., 30. WHITE MT: Gn., 13, 20.
S. CARLOS: Gd., 15–16; 34; (Cp. 79–80).
    *Killing of monster with arrow chase*         CHIR: Op., 10–11.
MESC: Hoij., 188; Op. ms. LIPAN: Op., 18–19, 28. JIC:
Mooney, 204–05; Op., 58–61. S. CARLOS: Gd., 35. This episode
is combined with the preceding one in the two Jicarilla versions.
    *Killing of eye-killers.*  CHIR: Hoij., 12–13; Op., (Cp. 10–11), (note
    2) 11.

MESC: Hoij., 187–88; Op., ms. LIPAN: Op. 21–22. JIC: Op., 75–76. NAV: Matth. (a), 222–23; Matth. (e), 123–24; Haile, 123; Newcomb and Reich., 31. WHITE MT: Gn., 25–26. S. CARLOS: Gd., 13, 33–34.

IB1b. *Origin of culture hero(es)—supernatural conception; Killing of monster eagles; Killing of giant.* (See IB1a.)

IB2. *Origin of food types* CHIR: Op., 14.
Compare IA1b. *Choice of culture types.*

IB3. *Origin of girl's puberty ceremony* CHIR: Op., 15.
MESC: Op., ms. JIC: Op., 49, 87–95. NAV: Curtis, 94–95; Fran. F., 355; Gd., 150–53; Haile, 85–91. WHITE MT: Gd., 123–24.

IB4. *Liberation of animals* CHIR: Op., 15–18.
MESC: Op., ms. LIPAN: Op., 122–25. JIC: Russ., 259–61; Gd., 212–13, 214; Op., 256–60. WHITE MT: Gd., 126–27; Gn., 86–88.

IB5. *(Big John and Little John)* CHIR: Op., 18–20.
See note 1, p. 18.

IB6. *(Departure of culture hero)* CHIR: Op., 20–21.
Since this story is the result of Christian influence (note 1, p. 20), it resembles only in a general way the other versions of the departure of heroes.

IC1. *Escape by simulating death* CHIR: Op., 21.
MESC: Op., ms. LIPAN: Op., 173. WHITE MT: Gn., (Cp. 183).

IC2. *Escape by grasping limb* CHIR: Op., 22.
MESC: Op., ms. LIPAN: Op., 59, 174. JIC: Op., 74–75. NAV: Parsons, 375. WHITE MT: Gd., 137–38; Gn. 183–84.
*Escape through fear of horned toad* CHIR: Op., 22.
MESC: Op., ms. LIPAN: Op., 60. NAV: Parsons, (Cp. 373). WHITE MT: Gn., 189.

IIA1a. *Contest for daylight* CHIR: Hoij., 14–16; Op., 23–25, 25–27.
MESC: Op., ms. LIPAN: Op., 87–94, 94–96. JIC: Mooney, 198; Gd., 207; Op., 231–34. NAV: Matth. (d), 4–6; Newcomb and Reich., 31. WESTERN APACHE (Tribe undesignated): Bourke, 211. WHITE MT: Gn., 148–49; 149–50. S. CARLOS: Gd., 43–44, 44.

IIA1b. *Contest for daylight* (See IIA1a.)
*Release of darkness* (See IIIB47.)

IIIA1. *Origin of death—sinking test* CHIR: Op., 28.
MESC: Op., (Cp. ms.). LIPAN: Op., 38–39, (Cp. 39–40). JIC: Russ., 258; Gd., 194; Op., 44–47, 268. NAV: Van Vleet, 71–72; Matth. (e), 77; Gd., 138. WHITE MT: Gd., 138; Gn., 177–78.

IIIB1. *Abandoned on growing rock* CHIR: Op., 28–30.
MESC: Op., ms. LIPAN: Op., 176. JIC: Gd., (Cp. 224); Op., 286. S. CARLOS: Gd., 67.

Theft of wife by trickster            CHIR: Op., 28–31.
MESC: Op., ms. LIPAN: Op., 127–30. JIC: Gd., 224; Op., 286–88.
WHITE MT: Gn., (Cp. 156–61). S. CARLOS: Gd., 67–68.

IIIB2. *Talking objects aid traveler*          CHIR: Op., 30–31, 100.
MESC: Op., ms. LIPAN: Op., 128. JIC: Russ., 260–61; Gd.,
224; Op., 259, 287–88. S. CARLOS: Gd., 67.

IIIB3. *Lecherous father*          CHIR: Hoij., 25–27; Op., 31–34.
MESC: Hoij., 182–83; Op., ms. LIPAN: Op., 135–36, 136–39.
JIC: Op., 280–82. NAV: Matth. (b), 271–73. WHITE MT: Gd.,
138; Gn., 152–54.

IIIB4. *Dummy mistaken for rabbit*          CHIR: Hoij., 19; Op., 34.
MESC: Op., ms. LIPAN: Op., 147, 147. JIC: Op., 299–300.
WHITE MT: Gn., 170.

IIIB5. *Rabbit mistaken for dummy*          CHIR: Hoij., 19–20; Op., 34.
MESC: Op., ms. LIPAN: 147, 147. WHITE MT: Gn., 170.

IIIB6. *Refuge disclosure promised—escape method*      CHIR: Op., 34–35.
*Escape through hollow log*          CHIR: Op., 35.
JIC: Op., 300–01.

IIIB7. *Moving rock insulted with excrement*   CHIR: Hoij., 20–21; Op., 35–36.
MESC: Op., ms. LIPAN: Op., 117, 121–22. JIC: Gd., 234; Op.,
324, 335–36.

IIIB8. *Voices from below—escape method*        CHIR: Hoij., 21; Op., 36.
MESC: Op., ms. LIPAN: Op., 148, 148–49. JIC: Op., 301–02.

IIIB9. *Holding up sky—escape method*     CHIR: Hoij., 21–22; Op., 36–37.
MESC: Op., ms. LIPAN: Op., 149–50, 150. JIC: Op., 279.
WHITE MT: Gn., 193, 199. S. CARLOS: Gd., 74–75. This inci-
dent is probably of European origin.

IIIB10. *Hoodwinked dancers*          CHIR: Hoij., 22–24; Op., 37–38.
MESC: Op., ms. LIPAN: Op., 151–52. JIC: Russ., 264; Gd.,
230; Op., 272–73. NAV: Parsons, (Cp. 372). WHITE MT: Gn.,
(Cp. 169–70). S. CARLOS: Gd., (Cp. 73).

IIIB11. *Theft of food during sleep*          CHIR: Hoij., 24: Op., 38–39.
MESC: Op., ms. LIPAN: Op., 152, 154–55. JIC: Russ., 264;
Gd., 230; Op., 273. NAV: Parsons, (Cp. 372).

IIIB12. *Diving for reflection*          CHIR: Op., 39, 67.
MESC: Op., ms. LIPAN: Op., 152–53; 155. JIC: Russ., 264; Gd.,
230; Op., 274, 332. NAV: Parsons, 374–75. WHITE MT: Gn.,
188. This idea also has an Old World and a Spanish-American
distribution; its presence in American Indian mythology may
well be due to white contact.

IIIB13. *Transformation trick*          CHIR: Op., 39–40.
MESC: Op., ms. LIPAN: Op., 154–56, 156. JIC: Russ., 264; Op.,
274. NAV: Parsons, 369. WHITE MT: Gn., 166–67.

IIIB14. *Fictitious ally—escape method*        CHIR: Hoij., 20; Op., 40.
MESC: Op., ms. JIC: Op., 299.

IIIB15. *Intercourse with mother-in-law* CHIR: Op., 40–41.
JIC: Op., 313–14.

IIIB16. *Escape up tree* CHIR: Op., 41, 68.
MESC: Op., ms. LIPAN: Op., 145. JIC: Gd., 233; Op., 292.
WHITE MT: Gn., 188. An episode in a story that originated in
the Old World.

IIIB17. *Bee container opened* CHIR: Op., 41–42
MESC: Op., ms. LIPAN: Op., 179–80. JIC: Russ., 267–68;
Op., 329–30. A Spanish-American incident.

IIIB18. *Bungling host—wings imitated* CHIR: Op., 42–43.
MESC: Op., ms. JIC: Gd., (Cp. 232–33); Op., (Cp. 276–77).

IIIB19. *Foolish imitation—children in line* CHIR: Op., 43.
MESC: Hoij., 182; Op., ms. LIPAN: Op., 186. JIC: Op., 292–93.
WHITE MT: Gn., 154.

IIIB20. *Bungling host—piercing nose for food* CHIR: Op., 44.
MESC: Op., ms. LIPAN: Op., 139–40. JIC: Russ., 266; Gd.,
232; Op., 275, 276. NAV: Matth. (e), 87.

IIIB21. *Bungling host—butting cliff for food* CHIR: Op., 45.
MESC: Op., (Cp. ms.). JIC: Op., (Cp. 307).

IIIB22. *Habitats reversed* CHIR: Op., 45–46.
MESC: Op., ms. LIPAN: Op., 159–61. JIC: Gd., 231; Op.,
312–13. NAV: Parsons, 370. WHITE MT: Gn., 167–68.

IIIB23. *Bungling host—food returned to bee* CHIR: Op., 46–47.
MESC: Op., ms. JIC: Op., 302–03.

IIIB24. *Bungling host—food from arrows in fire* CHIR: Op., 47.
JIC: Russ., 265–66. NAV: Matth. (e), 87–88.

IIIB25. *Trickster as herder kills animals* CHIR: Op., 47.
MESC: Op., ms. LIPAN: Op., 166. WHITE MT: Gd., (Cp.
138); Gn., 200–01.

*False message leads to adultery* CHIR: Op., 48.
MESC: Op., ms. LIPAN: Op., (note 1) 166, (Cp. 177). WHITE
MT: Gn., 187.

*Trick—intoxication* CHIR: Op., 48–49.
LIPAN: Op., 165, 190. European influence is apparent in the
three episodes above. The first, especially, suggests the Spanish
*Pedro Urdimales* cycle.

IIIB26. *Fraud—money tree* CHIR: Hoij., 18–19; Op., 49–50.
MESC: Op., ms. LIPAN: Op. 164. WHITE MT: Gn., 195. A
Spanish-American tale.

IIIB27. *Fraud—hat contents* CHIR: Op., 51.
WHITE MT: Gn., 196–97. Another Spanish-American tale.

IIIB28. *Theft of fire—tail torch* CHIR: Hoij., 17–18; Op., 51–53.
MESC: Op., ms. LIPAN: Op., 109–11, 111–14. JIC: Russ.,
261–62; Curtis, 69; Gd., 208–09, 209; Op., 269–72. NAV: Newcomb and Reich., (Cp. 31). WESTERN APACHE (Tribe undesignated): Bourke, (Cp. 212). WHITE MT: Gn., 147–48.
S. CARLOS: Gd., 41–42, 43.

IIIB29. *Intercourse at distance*                                    CHIR: Op., 53–54.
MESC: Op., ms. LIPAN: Op., 186–87, 187–89, 189.

IIIB30. *Eye juggler*                                                CHIR: Op., 54.
MESC: Op., ms. LIPAN: Op., 171, 171–73. JIC: Gd., 229; Op.,
(Cp. 238), 277–78. NAV: Matth. (e), 89–90. WHITE MT:
Gn., 161–62. S. CARLOS: Gd., 73.

IIIB31. *Dance with reeds*                                           CHIR: Op., 54.
MESC: Op., ms. LIPAN: Op., 181. WHITE MT: Gn., 162.

IIIB32. *Blind trickster*                                            CHIR: Op., 54–56.
MESC: Op., ms. NAV: Matth. (e), 90–91. WHITE MT: Gn.,
162–63.

IIIB33. *Added equipment*                      CHIR: Op., 56–57, (note 1) 57.
LIPAN: Op., 166–67. JIC: Op., 316–17. WHITE MT: Gn.,
193–94.

*Fraud—painted animal*                  CHIR: Op., 57, (note 2) 57.
LIPAN: Op., 167. WHITE MT: Gn., 194–95. The two episodes
above may be European in origin.

IIIB34. *Substitute victim*                                          CHIR: Op., 57–58.
MESC: Op., ms. LIPAN: Op., 180–81. JIC: Russ., 268. WHITE
MT: Gn., 191, 198. S. CARLOS: Gd., 74. This is a Spanish-
American incident; it often occurs as a part of the *Tar Baby*
story.

IIIB35. *Trickster disturbs rats*                                    CHIR: Op., 58.

IIIB36. *Killing while pretending to cure*     CHIR: Op., 58–60, (note 2) 65.
MESC: Op., ms. LIPAN: Op., 178–79. JIC: Op., 327–29.
WHITE MT: Gn., 155–56.

IIIB37. *Little rabbits sing*                                        CHIR: Op., 60–61.

IIIB38. *Leg mutilation*                         CHIR: Op., 61, (note 1) 61.
MESC: Op., ms. LIPAN: Op., 174–75. JIC: Russ., 262; Gd.,
225; Op., 289, 289. NAV: Matth. (e), 91–93. WHITE MT: Gn.,
174–75.

IIIB39. *Trickster crushes birds*                                    CHIR: Op., 61.
*Intercourse attempted through stumbling*               CHIR: Op., 61.

IIIB40. *Boy passes as girl*                                         CHIR: Op., 61–62.
JIC: Gd., (Cp. 235). See IIIB41.

IIIB41. *Boy passes as girl—theft of tobacco*            CHIR: Op., 62–63.
MESC: Op., ms. JIC: Op., 294–95. WHITE MT: Gn., 151–52.
See IIIB40.

IIIB42. *Killing with heated rocks*            CHIR: Op., (note 2) 28, 63–64.
MESC: Op., ms. LIPAN: Op., 126, 130. JIC: Gd., 224; Op.,
288. NAV: Wyman, 137. WHITE MT: Gd., 132. S. CARLOS:
Gd., 68.

IIIB43. *Fall from tree toilet* (See IIIB49).

IIIB44. *Ways of life compared—coyote and dog*          CHIR: Op., 64–65.
MESC: Op., ms. LIPAN: Op., 192. JIC: Op., 330–31. Cp.
IIIC2.

IIIB45. *Trickster eats forbidden food* CHIR: Op., 65, 71.
LIPAN: Op., 115–16, 116, 119. JIC: Op., 279–80, 303–04.
WHITE MT: Gn., 172–73.

IIIB46. *Guarded weapon materials* CHIR: Op., 65–66, (note 2) 65.
MESC: Op., ms. LIPAN: Op., (Cp. 115). JIC: Gd., (Cp. 203).
WHITE MT: Gn., 12, (Cp. 20). S. CARLOS: Gd., (Cp. 12).
Animal and supernatural guardians occur in many other contexts in Apachean mythology.

IIIB47. *Release of darkness* CHIR: Op., (note 1) 27, 66.
MESC: Op., ms. WHITE MT: Gn., 164–65.

IIIB48. *Travel inside an animal* CHIR: Op., 66.
MESC: Op., ms. LIPAN: Op., 142–43. JIC: Russ., 263; Gd.,
228; Op., 258–59, 282–83. WHITE MT: Gn., 118–19.

IIIB49. *Contest—jumping for meat* CHIR: Op., 66–67.
MESC: Op., (Cp. ms). LIPAN: Op., (Cp. 120, 143). JIC: Russ.,
263; Gd., 228; Op., 283–84. NAV: Parsons, (Cp. 372).

*Killing by throwing bone* CHIR., Op. 67.
MESC: Op., ms. JIC: Russ., 263; Gd., 229; Op., 284–85. WHITE
MT: Gn., 119.

*Fall from tree toilet* CHIR: Op., 64, 67.
MESC: Op., ms. JIC: Russ., 263–64; Gd., 229; Op., 285.

IIIB50. *Diving for reflection* (See IIIB12.)
*Escape up tree* (See IIIB16.)

IIIB51. *Visit to ant and mouse people* CHIR: Op., 68–69.

IIIB52. *Foolish counting* CHIR: Op., 69.
JIC: Op., (Cp. 308–09).

IIIB53. *False message—escape method* CHIR: Op., 69.
MESC: Op., ms. LIPAN: Op., 144–45. JIC: Gd., 233; Op., 291.
NAV: Parsons, 374. WHITE MT: Gn., 186–88. A European
incident?

IIIB54. *Bearskin quiver causes trouble* CHIR: Op., 69–70.
MESC: Op., ms. JIC: Op., 326–27. WHITE MT: Gn., 172–73.

IIIB55. *Toothed vagina made harmless* CHIR: Op., 70.
JIC: Gd., 203; Op., 67–70. WHITE MT: Gn., 21–22, 39. S.
CARLOS: Gd., 14–15, 32–33.

IIIB56. *Foolish imitation—spots on children* CHIR: Op., 70–71.
MESC: Op., ms. LIPAN: Op., 141, 141–42. JIC: Russ., 265;
Gd., 227; Op., 285–86. NAV: Parsons, 371. WHITE MT: Gn.,
155.

IIIB57. *Trickster eats forbidden food* (See IIIB45.)

IIIB58. *Trickster flies with birds* CHIR: Op., 71.
MESC: Op., ms. LIPAN: Op., 108–09. JIC: Russ., 261; Op.,
292.

*(Trickster blinded and burned)* CHIR: Op., 71–72.
JIC: Russ., 267; Op., 234–38. A fragment of a Spanish-American
story.

*Reversed moccasins rationalized* CHIR: Op., 72.
Cp. Bear's reversal of moccasins in most Apachean versions of
the *Contest for daylight* (IIA1a.).
*Intercourse by disguise* CHIR: Op., 72.
*Serial dismemberment* CHIR: Op., 72.
MESC: Op., ms. JIC: Op., 355–57.
*Trickster attempts cattle riding* CHIR: Op., 72.
IIIC1. *Journey of geese* CHIR: Op., 72.
MESC: Op., ms. Cp. IIIB58. *Trickster flies with birds.*
IIIC2. *Ways of life compared—rat and mouse* CHIR: Op., 72–73.
LIPAN: Op., 203. Cp. IIIB44.
IIIC3. *Way of life—robber fly* CHIR: Op., 73.
IVA1. *Curing of blind and lame* CHIR: Hoij., 35; Op., 74–75.
MESC: Op., ms. LIPAN: Op., 50–51. NAV: Matth. (f), (Cp.
170–71), 209–10, 212–65. WHITE MT: Gn., (Cp. 111), 112–13.
IVA2. *Origin of Masked Dancer Ceremony* CHIR: Hoij., 27–28; Op.,
75–76.
*Revenge by offended supernaturals* CHIR: Hoij., 28–30; Op., 76–78.
MESC: Op., (Cp. ms.).
IVA3. *Supernaturals defeat enemy (Mexicans)* CHIR: Op., 78.
MESC: Op., ms.
IVA4. *Supernaturals participate in ceremony* CHIR: Hoij., 30–33;
Op., 78–79.
IVB1. *Abduction by water monster* CHIR: Hoij., 42; Op., 79–80, 80–81.
MESC: Op., ms. LIPAN: Op., (Cp. 62). JIC: Mooney, (Cp.
201–03); Curtis, (Cp. 64–65); Gd., (Cp. 199–200, 200–01); Op.,
(Cp. 104–09). NAV: Matth. (e), 73–74; Haile, (Cp. 127–29).
IVB2. *Abduction by water monster* (See IVB1.)
IVC1. *Visit to dead* CHIR: Op., 82, 83.
LIPAN: Op., (Cp. 41–42, 47–48), 97–98, 98–100, 100–01, 101–04,
104–05.
VA1. *Ignorance of horses' habits* CHIR: Hoij., 37, 39; Op., 84, 86.
MESC: Op., ms. LIPAN: Op., 205–06. JIC: Op., 360.
*Reversed riding* CHIR: Hoij., 37; Op., 84.
MESC: Op., ms. LIPAN: Op., 206. JIC: Op., 357–59.
VA2. *Calling like crows during intercourse* CHIR: Hoij., 36, 39; Op.,
84, 86.
MESC: Op., ms. LIPAN: Op., 211.
VA3. *Foolish searchers* CHIR: Hoij., 35, 39; Op., 85, 86.
LIPAN: Op., 208.
VA4. *Worthless trophy* CHIR: Hoij., 38; Op., 85.
MESC: Op., ms. LIPAN: Op., 205.
VA5. *Thrown entrails amuse enemy* CHIR: Hoij., 39–40; Op., 85.
VA6. *Unrecognized hostility* CHIR: Hoij., 37; Op., 85, 86.
MESC: Op., ms. LIPAN: Op., 206, 209–10. JIC: Op., 364.
VA7. *Hooves mistaken for rocks* CHIR: Hoij., 39; Op., 86.
JIC: Op., 359–60.

*Ignorance of horses' habits* (See VA1.)
*Unintended victim—man for insect*    CHIR: Hoij., 39; Op., 86.
JIC: Op., 362.
*Foolish searchers* (See VA3.)
*Unrecognized hostility* (See VA6.)
*Calling like crows during intercourse* (See VA2.)

VB1. *Infidelity after pretended death*    CHIR: Op., 87.
LIPAN: Op., 213–17. JIC: Op., 371–73. Compare IIIB3. *Lecherous father.*

VB2. *Infidelity during pretended sickness*    CHIR: Op., 87, 87–89.
MESC: Op., ms. LIPAN: Op., 217–19. JIC: Op., 264–65.
WHITE MT: Gn., 142–44.

VB3. *Infidelity during pretended sickness* (See VB2.)

VC1. *Sexual use of cactus*    CHIR: Op., 89.
MESC: Op., ms. JIC: Op., 369–70. NAV: Matth. (e), (Cp. 107);
Gd., (Cp. 155); Haile, (Cp. 77).

VD1. *Trick—quarrel instigated*    CHIR: Op., 89–90.
MESC: Op., ms. LIPAN: Op., 185. JIC: Russ., 269; Op., 314–16.
*Unintended victim—man for bone*    CHIR: Op., 90.
*Trick—luring over bank*    CHIR: Op., 90.
LIPAN: Op., 185.

VI1. *Legs fed with grease*    CHIR: Op., 91.
MESC: Op., ms. LIPAN: Op., 288.

VI2. *Despised boy*    CHIR: Op., 91.
MESC: Op., ms. LIPAN: Op. 288. JIC: Op. (Mem. Amer. Anth.
Assoc. 52), 5–80, Op., 384–87. NAV: Matth. (c), 411–17.

VI3. *Eagle trained to hunt*    CHIR: Op., 91–92.
MESC: Op., ms.

VI4. *The magic ring*    CHIR: Hoij., 43–45; Op ., 92–95.
WHITE MT: Gn., 209–15.

VI5. *Quarrel between wind and rain (thunder)*    CHIR: Hoij., 16–17;
Op., 95–96.
LIPAN: Op., 86. JIC: Op., 78–79, 216. WHITE MT: Gn., (Cp.
122).

VI6a. *Sacred book destroyed*    CHIR: Op., 96, 96–97.
VI6b. *Sacred book destroyed* (See VI6a.)

VI7. *Origin of old age—unfulfilled tasks*    CHIR: Op., 98–99.

VI8. *Killing of monster eagles* (See IB1a.)
*Talking objects aid traveler* (See IIIB2.)

VI9. *Destruction of earth*    CHIR: Op., 100.
JIC: Op., (Cp. 111, 112–13). NAV: Packard, (Cp. 85); Stevenson, (Cp. 279); Parsons, (Cp. 370–71).

VI10. *Visitor attacked by pet eagle*    CHIR: Op., 101.
MESC: Op., ms.
*Visit to sky with birds (eagles)*    CHIR: Op., 101.
JIC: Gd., 210–12; Op., 100–04, 376–78. NAV: Matth. (e), 195–208; Reich., 26–36. WHITE MT: Gd., 132–35. S. CARLOS:
Gd., 67–68.

# BIBLIOGRAPHY

John G. Bourke, Notes on Apache Mythology, *Journal of American Folk-Lore*, 3 (1890), 209–212.

L. H. Dudley Buxton, Some Navajo Folktales and Customs, *Folk-Lore*, 34 (1923), 239–313.

Edward F. Castetter and M. E. Opler, *The Ethnobiology of the Chiricahua and Mescalero Apache*, Bulletin of the University of New Mexico, Albuquerque: University of New Mexico Press, 1936.

Edward Curtis, *The North American Indian*, Cambridge: University Press, 1907, Vol. 1.

The Franciscan Fathers, *An Ethnologic Dictionary of the Navaho Language*, St. Michaels, Arizona, 1910.

Pliny Earle Goddard, *Jicarilla Apache Texts*, Anthropological Papers of the American Museum of Natural History, 8, 1911.

    *Myths and Tales from the San Carlos Apache*, Anthropological Papers of the American Museum of Natural History, 24, Part 1, 1918, 1–86.

    *Myths and Tales from the White Mountain Apache*, Anthropological Papers of the American Museum of Natural History, 24, Part 2, 1919, 87–139.

    *Navajo Texts*, Anthropological Papers of the American Museum of Natural History, 34, Part 1, 1933, 1–179.

Grenville Goodwin, *Myths and Tales of the White Mountain Apache*, Memoir of the American Folk-Lore Society, 33, New York: J. J. Augustin, 1939.

Father Berard Haile, *Origin Legend of the Navaho Enemy Way*, Yale University Publications in Anthropology, 17, New Haven: Yale University Press, 1938.

Harry Hoijer, *Chiricahua and Mescalero Apache Texts*, with Ethnological Notes by Morris Edward Opler, Chicago: University of Chicago Press 1938.

Weston La Barre, *The Peyote Cult*, Yale University Publications in Anthropology, 19, New Haven: Yale University Press, 1938.

Washington Matthews, (a) A Part of the Navajo's Mythology, *American Antiquarian*, 5, No. 3 (1883), 207–224.

    (b) The Origin of the Utes, A Navajo Myth, *American Antiquarian*, 7, No. 5 (1885), 271–274.

    (c) The Mountain Chant: A Navajo Ceremony, *Fifth Annual Report of the Bureau of American Ethnology*, Washington, 1887, 379–467.

    (d) Navajo Gambling Songs, *American Anthropologist* (Old Series), 2, No. 1 (1889), 1–19.

    (e) *Navaho Legends*, Memoir of the American Folk-Lore Society, 5, New York, G. E. Stechert and Co., 1897.

    (f) *The Night Chant, A Navaho Ceremony*, Memoir of the American Museum of Natural History, 6, 1902.

James Mooney, The Jicarilla Genesis, *American Anthropologist* (Old Series), 11, No. 7 (1898), 197–209.

Franc J. Newcomb and Gladys A. Reichard, *Sandpaintings of the Navajo Shooting Chant*, New York: J. J. Augustin, 1938.

Morris Edward Opler, The Concept of Supernatural Power among the Chiricahua and Mescalero Apaches, *American Anthropologist*, 37, No. 1 (1935), 65–70.

An Interpretation of Ambivalence of Two American Indian Tribes, *Journal of Social Psychology*, 7 (1936), 82–116.

Some Points of Comparison and Contrast between the Treatment of Functional Disorders by Apache Shamans and Modern Psychiatric Practice, *American Journal of Psychiatry*, 92, No. 6 (1936), 1371–1387.

The Kinship Systems of the Southern Athabaskan-Speaking Tribes: A Comparative Study, *American Anthropologist*, 38, No. 4 (1936), 620–633.

An Outline of Chiricahua Apache Social Organization, in *Social Anthropology* (Edited by Fred Eggan), Chicago: University of Chicago Press, 1937. 173–239.

*Myths and Tales of the Jicarilla Apache Indians*, Memoir of the American Folk-Lore Society, 31, New York: G. E. Stechert and Co., 1938.

The Sacred Clowns of the Chiricahua and Mescalero Apache Indians, *El Palacio*, 44 (1938), 75–79.

*Dirty Boy: A Jicarilla Tale of Raid and War*, Memoir of the American Anthropological Association, 52, 1938.

Further Comparative Anthropological Data Bearing on the Solution of a Psychological Problem, *Journal of Social Psychology*, 9 (1938), 477–483.

Humor and Wisdom of Some American Indian Tribes, *New Mexico Anthropologist*, 3 (1938), 3–10.

A Chiricahua Apache's Account of the Geronimo Campaign of 1886, *New Mexico Historical Review*, 8, No. 4 (1938), 360–386.

*Myths and Legends of the Lipan Apache Indians*, Memoir of the American Folk-Lore Society, 36, New York: J. J. Augustin, 1940.

The Raid and War-Path Language of the Chiricahua Apache (with Harry Hoijer), *American Anthropologist*, 42, No. 4 (1940), 617–634.

Three Types of Variation and their Relation to Culture Change, in *Language, Culture, and Personality: Essays in Memory of Edward Sapir* (ed. Leslie Spier, A. Irving Hallowell, and Stanley S. Newman), Menasha: Banta, 1941.

*An Apache Life-Way:* the Economic, Social, and Religious Institutions of the Chiricahua Indians, Chicago: University of Chicago Press, 1941.

*Myths and Tales of the Mescalero Apache Indians*, ms.

R. L. Packard, A Navajo Myth, *Transactions of the Anthropological Society of Washington*, 1 (1882), 84–85.

Elsie Clews Parsons, Navaho Folktales, *Journal of American Folk-Lore*, 36 (1923), 368–375.

Gladys A. Reichard, *Navajo Medicine Man*, New York: J. J. Augustin, 1939. See also: Franc J. Newcomb and Gladys A. Reichard.

Frank Russell, Myths of the Jicarilla Apache, *Journal of American Folk-Lore*, 11 (1898), 253–271.

A. M. Stephen, (a) The Navajo, *American Anthropologist* (Old Series), 6, No. 4 (1893), 345–362.

(b) Navajo Origin Legend, *Journal of American Folk-Lore*, 43 (1930), 88–104.

James Stevenson, Ceremonial of Hasjelti Dailjis and Mythical Sand Painting of the Navajo Indians, *Eighth Annual Report of the Bureau of American Ethnology*, Washington, 1891, 229–285.

T. Stanton Van Vleet, Legendary Evolution of the Navajo Indians, *American Naturalist*, 27 (1893), 69–79.

Leland C. Wyman, Origin Legends of Navaho Divinatory Rites, *Journal of American Folk-Lore*, 49 (1936), 134–142.

IN THE SOURCES OF AMERICAN INDIAN ORAL LITERATURE SERIES

*Myths and Traditions of the Crow Indians*
by Robert H. Lowie

*Myths and Tales of the Chiricahua Apache Indians*
by Morris Edward Opler

*Myths and Tales of the Jicarilla Apache Indians*
by Morris Edward Opler